What Every Conservative Should Know About Communism

Lyndon H. LaRouche, Jr.

The New Benjamin Franklin House
Publishing Company
New York

OTHER BOOKS BY LYNDON H. LAROUCHE, JR.

Dialectical Economics

The Case of Walter Lippmann

The Power of Reason—A Kind of an Autobiography

How to Defeat Liberalism and William F. Buckley

Will the Soviets Rule in the 1980s?

Basic Economics for Conservative Democrats

What Every Conservative Should Know
About Communism
Published by The New Benjamin Franklin House
Publishing Company, Inc.
Copyright © 1980 by Lyndon H. LaRouche, Jr.

FIRST EDITION

For information address the publisher:
The New Benjamin Franklin House
Publishing Company, Inc.
304 West 58th St.
New York 10019

ISBN: 0-933488-06-8
Cover photo: Culver Pictures
Cover design by Alan Yue

PRINTED IN THE UNITED STATES OF AMERICA

CONTENTS

Preface

There are two different species among those Americans who accept the label of "conservative." The two are as different from one another as people differ from radialarian ooze.

The one variety is an unwholesome breed of pot-puffing fops, thugs, and faggots, of the sort one might expect to find at any convening of New York's East Side Conservative Club. From William Buckley, Roy Cohn, William Safire on, a nastier, more debased lot of loyal scoundrels for Her Majesty the Queen would be hard to discover.

The more numerous, opposing species of "conservative" is a continuation of what was formerly hated by the British aristocracy, and named "American nationalists." General Douglas MacArthur is usually prominent on the list of heroes for such folk. The more literate among them are distinguished by fairly detailed knowledge of the treasonous character of the New York Council on Foreign Relations, "Bilderbergers," and the Trilateral Commission.

Most of the inner kernel among the second sort

of patriotic conservative reads the weekly *Spotlight,* and a fair proportion have also read W. Cleon Skousen's *The Naked Capitalist,* as well as despising the pot-puffing Yale fop William F. Buckley. This kernel is, so to speak, the "Gideon's Army" of American nationalism today, up to a quarter-million more influential persons who are the opinion leaders for a similarly inclined population more than a scorefold larger. At least, that is a fair country estimate of the matter.

When it comes to the subject of "communism," the better-informed among these nationalists start out from soundly documented proof of the roles of the Morgans, the Rothschilds, the Warburgs, the Schiffs, arguing, quite correctly, that such "communism" is a product of the same crew standing behind the "one-world" effort more generally. Beyond that factually grounded point in their analysis, most of those nationalists have tended to go over the edge into unsubstantiable further conclusions.

Skousen's *The Naked Capitalist* is one of the best versions of that skewed analysis in general circulation from the ranks of the nationalists. That book, plus the gist of the view offered by *Spotlight,* are the principal reference points from which the following pages work to provide a corrected overview of the business of communism.

The purpose, in brief, is summed up in the simple slogan: *Better informed is better armed.*

With the ushering in of fascist totalitarianism by the Carter administration, the United States urgently needs better-informed antitotalitarian patriots.

Now, a few words about the purpose of this short work.

Although the following pages are directed to a specific minority among self-styled "conservatives," it is intended that many others should read this same material, as if viewing the exchange from "over the shoulders" of both the writer and the members of the audience to which this is most specifically addressed.

The basic constituency for the writer's point of view includes the sort of conservative identified above. It also includes more-numerous portions of the electorate. These are met among professionals dedicated to scientific and technological progress. They are met among entrepreneurs, including owner-operater farmers whose instinctive productive practice fulfills in important part Alexander Hamilton's 1791 *Report to the Congress On The Subject of Manufactures;* are met among trade-unionists dedicated to the principle of a fair profit and fair wage; and among what has been termed over the last decade and a half that portion of the "black" minority that moved from the Republican into the Democratic Party during the 1928-1936 period. All of these named strata might be termed "conservative,' in the sense that they, wittingly or otherwise, perpetuate the world-outlook associated with the Whig Party of the early nineteenth century.

That combination of witting and "organic" Whig Americans represents potentially about 75 percent of the adult electorate. This is concentrated, by age-groups, among that portion of the adult population over thirty-five—Vietnam War veteran ages on up, through those who reached or had reached adulthood by the time of the Second World War.

Underneath, those actual and potential Whigs share a common morality. From the experiences of electoral campaigning and related opportunities, I have been able to formulate the common ground of that morality in the following terms. I now summarize that tested statement of a common morality, and with aid of that clarification, conclude this preface by identifying the larger purpose to which it is directed among all the proposed readers, both the indicated "conservatives" and those others who follow—"over their shoulders."

American Whig Morality

The person who is truly moral begins from the fact that he or she is born and must someday die. That person is therefore informed in conscience to regard that ephemeral, mortal existence as a totality: "What shall I do with this mortal life as a whole, that its being lived has some broader, enduring meaning? How do I give it meaning, beyond moment-to-moment gratification of sensual appetites and pursuit of such exotic entertainments as might relieve the boredom and the jaded appetites of the moment before?"

Moral citizens most frequently express that morality concretely in terms of their children, grandchildren, and other members of our national posterity more generally. They say to their children and grandchildren: "Develop your mind, make something of your life, using the opportunities we have lived and worked to help make available to you." They say: "Live a life of which you need not be ashamed."

This morality is efficiently typified by comparing the outlook of that sort of American farmer who has made our agriculture the most productive in the world, to the debased outlook of the spokesman for the "hippie rural commune." The way in which the productive, owner-operator farmer has used such aids as the agricultural extension service, using industrial products and technology, to fulfill the American System as outlined in Hamilton's *On The Subject of Manufactures,* expresses in the exemplary practical way the sort of morality we have summarized above. The "hippie" revives the degraded ways of the serfs of Sodom and Gomorrah.

That which is *divine,* that power of perfectible creative intelligence which Apostolic Christianity identifies as the "image of God" in man, is expressed by the search not only to discover the lawful ordering of the universe more perfectly. One must govern one's conscience in daily practice by the zeal to perfect and celebrate in practice those creative-mental powers which express the divine, which express the fundamental distinction of man over the "Malthusian", "zero technological growth" policy of all species of beasts.

We moral citizens hate the morality of the "hippies," smelling the evil which that morality reflects. "Cultural relativism," whether as the debased, racialist doctrine of "negritude," or as a policy of beastlike submission to a heathen pantheist's notion of "natural nature," defines man morally as a beast of Darwinian biology.

These beasts, men and women who degrade themselves into beastlikeness, do not view their mortal lives as entireties. Instead, they act out their irrational impulses, their appetites, their fleeting prejudices, from moment to moment, without a sense of moral purpose for the outcome of their lives as wholes.

The morality of *Playboy* magazine is evil, not simply because it represents the policy of Sodom and Gomorrah, but because the essence of pornography is an animallike life lived from momentary sensual impulse to the next such impulsive moment. It is pragmatism, otherwise the moral indifferentism of David Hume's empiricism, the hedonism or utilitarianism of Jeremy Bentham and

John Stuart Mill, which expresses the evil of Sodom and Gomorrah. *Playboy* is evil, not because it is pornography, but because pornography is an instrument of psychological warfare on behalf of hedonism-utilitarianism. It is being a pragmatist, being dominated by moment-to-moment "practical" considerations, that is the essential wickedness, evil.

The Purpose of These Pages
The possibility of saving the United States from the self-destruction, the imminent suicide toward which the Carter administration has accelerated us, depends upon pulling together the greater part of that approximate three-quarters of the electorate which is responsive to the kind of morality we have summarized above.

The patriot of the indicated "conservative" strata we are addressing most immediately in these pages is one, important constituent of that urgently needed electorate majority.

It is my duty to detect in the ranks of those conservatives, as for each other constituent of that potential majority, those accommodations to misinformation which prevent that stratum from deploying its forces effectively in fellowship and common purpose with other sectors of the indicated majority.

As will become clear over the course of the following pages, the disorientation among the conservatives is centered around a misevaluation of the matter of "communism." The problem is not that they are "anticommunists," but that their anticommunism is naive and counter-productive in respect of the very purposes which impel them to adopt anticommunism. They have substituted the negativism of naive anticommunism for a lack of clarity concerning the history of Christendom, a lack of clarity respecting the purposes for which this federal constitutional republic was created, and respecting the actual means by which it was brought into being.

The general problem of the still-moral majority of our nation's electorate, the conservative component most emphatically included, is that that morality has retreated into a Sunday exercise, has retreated from efficient expression in weekday life. In practical life, most otherwise moral citizens act as pragmatists, and create for themselves the consoling illusions which serve as apologies for a continuation of the moral antagonism between the two aspects of their total practice.

My task is to bring morality into the arena of day-to-day practice, to show how the world is actually organized in terms of that perspective. I must aid my fellow citizens of various identifiable strata in seeing how morality can be made efficient in day-to-day practice. To do so, I must also expose, even ridicule, those popularized illusions that take the place of comprehension today.

As those who are not self-defined "conservatives" join in overhearing the dialogue with "conservatives" over the course of the following pages, perhaps they, the onlookers, will be helped to see in themselves some likeness to the disabling problems which afflict the "conservatives."

Lyndon Hermyle LaRouche, Jr.
Wiesbaden, West Germany
April 8, 1980

1

CARTER USHERS IN FASCISM

Almost unopposed, except for the limited opposition rallied among my more immediate collaborators and supporters, the Carter administration has effected drastic alterations in the institutions of the United States, most emphatically over the period from the onset of the sabotage incident at the Three Mile Island nuclear-energy installation, during March 1979, through the March 1980 passage of a bill initiated by Representative Henry Reuss of Wisconsin, giving dictatorial powers to the Board of Governors of the Federal Reserve System.

The first action was the deploying of the Federal Emergency Management Agency (FEMA) exactly one day before the Three Mile Island sabotage went into effect. This agency's installation represents a profound change in the institutions of federal government, and is analogous in effect to the *allgemeine Notstandsgesätze* added to the law of Weimar Germany, enabling the 1933-1934 "legal coup d'état" which established Nazi Germany.

The concluding act of the cited period, initiated by Reuss, not only awards the Fed's Board of Governors arbitrary powers over all matters pertaining to public and private credit of the United States, but places included powers of the dictatorial FEMA under the direction of that same Board of Governors. In effect, the President and Congress of the United States have ended the sovereignty of the republic, surrendering dictatorial powers over the nation to a supranational, private agency, the London-coordinated International Monetary Fund.

In addition, the Carter administration has copiously perpetrated violations of felony laws in a dictatorial fashion, far exceeding anything of which the Nixon administration was accused even by its most extravagant critics of the "Watergate" proceedings period. Carter has used the Department of Justice, and elements of intelligence services mandated only to conduct foreign operations, for unlawful, dictatorial measures in our nation's domestic affairs, including the rigging of primary elections on a scale which is an order of magnitude beyond any precedent for election fraud in recent memory. The "color" of national emergency has been employed, in the most grossly felonious manner, not only to commit crimes, but to induce elements of the judiciary and other governmental agencies to condone such criminalities.

In brief, during this indicated period, *the Carter*

administration has led the United States into the first phase of becoming a fascist, totalitarian state, while also surrendering the sovereignty of the republic to a foreign, supranational entity.

This has occurred with aid of what amounts to Carter's "Reichstag Fire," the Carter administration's complicity in orchestrating and exploiting the taking of U.S. citizens hostage through terrorist acts by the Khomeini dictatorship of Iran.

The following are the "hard facts" of the matter.

In cooperation with the governments of the United Kingdom, Israel, and Communist China, the Carter administration implemented the doctrine of "Islamic fundamentalism," beginning in January 1978, not only to the end of bringing the lunatic Ayatollah Ruhollah Khomeini to power. It utilized the resources of the British Arab Bureau's "Muslim Brotherhood," to undertake the destabilization of a range of nations with Islamic populations, including India, Pakistan, Afghanistan, Iran, Turkey, Iraq, Syria, Lebanon, Jordan, Saudi Arabia, and large sections of Africa as well.

This use of the Muslim Brotherhood was adopted as part of the so-called Bernard Lewis Plan. That scheme was designed by British intelligence. Bernard Lewis, a key figure of British intelligence's Arab Bureau, was seconded to the U.S. intelligence community, in cooperation with a British intelligence front-organization, the Aspen Institute. Through the sponsorship of the Aspen

Institute, and cooperation of the Center for Strategic and International Studies of Georgetown University, the British scheme was conduited, with aid of Henry A. Kissinger, into the Carter administration. Zbigniew Brzezinski exercised his notorious flair for the exotic by labeling the scheme the "Arc of Crisis" policy, adding the subtitle, "Islamic fundamentalism" for the edification of certain strata of American Protestants.

The first phase of implementation of this "Arc of Crisis" doctrine was the manipulation of Arab-Israeli negotiations during 1977, to produce the cosmetic arrangement known popularly as the Camp David agreements. Underneath the cover of the publicized Camp David agreements were a set of secret agreements, overlapping matching secret agreements negotiated with the government of Communist China.

Under this nest of secret agreements, Communist China, Israel, Britain, and the United States deployed the Muslim Brotherhood and other chess-pieces to the included end of bringing Khomeini to power in Iran.

One of the prominently included features of the overall operation in the Islamic region was the creation of petroleum shortages. This "crisis management" of petroleum supplies was coordinated under the leadership of the London-based petroleum-marketing cartel, led by British Petroleum, Royal Dutch Shell, and Hermann Schmidt of

Mobil, and employing the cartel-controlled Rotterdam spot market to rig world-market oil prices. The principal targets of this petroleum blackmail were France, West Germany, and Japan. However, the petroleum hoax was also used by the Carter administration to effect the implementation of that administration's "energy policy": *the technological devolution of the economy of the United States.*

Once Khomeini had been brought to power, chiefly by the Carter administration's neutralization of Khomeini's opponents and arming of the Khomeiniacs, the second phase of the Iran operation was put into motion—the taking of U.S. citizens hostage by the Khomeini dictatorship.

This involved, prominently, former U.S. Attorney General Ramsey Clark. Clark, deeply involved in coordinating urban riot capabilities inside the United States, is a principal figure behind the organization of both legal and political support for such international terrorist groups as the West German Baader-Meinhof gang and Italy's Red Brigades. Clark was a key official Carter administration plenipotentiary representative in bringing Khomeini to power. Clark has also been involved, still as a Carter administration agent, in orchestrating the taking and coordination of U.S. citizens hostage in Iran. *Those are simply hard facts.*

Notable is the fact that the group of "students" holding the hostages are drawn chiefly from a combination of former students of Professor Norman Forer of Kansas University, plus members of a British-Israeli intelligence-controlled Palestinian group attached to the Palestine Liberation Organization. (Elements of Israeli intelligence have been controllers of sections of the Muslim Brotherhood since prior to the establishment of the state of Israel, and have controlled elements of Palestinian "terrorists" used repeatedly to create incidents against Israelis whenever Israeli government policy required such incidents for political purposes.) Forer, for example, has selected "suitable" religious figures and other delegations for invitation to Iran by the Khomeini dictatorship and the "students."

During the summer of 1979, in the course of exchanges on this and related matters, a State Department document was issued over the signature of Secretary Cyrus Vance. This document reported the view that it was probable that return of the exiled Shah to the United States would cause a taking of U.S. citizens hostage by the Khomeini dictatorship.

Under visible pressure from Henry A. Kissinger, and Kissinger's traveling checkbook, David Rockefeller, the State Department did admit the Shah into the United States. No measures were taken to provide for adequate security of U.S. consulates or the embassy in Iran; no alternative measures were taken to secure the safety of U.S. citizens placed in jeopardy.

From the taking of the hostages, itself an act of aggravated belligerency and terrorism against the United States, the Carter administration has responded chiefly by publicly soliciting an alliance with the Khomeini dictatorship. This has continued from the initial taking of the hostages to the Easter holidays. That policy is tantamount to treason according to the plain language of the Constitution; that policy has been exploited to manipulate the internal political affairs of the United States in several important ways, as well as to attempt blackmail against U.S. allies.

It has appeared more recently that Carter himself has been unable to exert efficient control over his nominal puppets of the Khomeini dictatorship. During February, he attempted to secure the confirmed release of the hostages for February 24, 1980—two days prior to the New Hampshire primary election. That not only failed, but aggravated the jeopardy of the hostages. Carter attempted a series of similar, subsequent efforts, each timed to coincide with a primary campaign event. This concluded with Carter's fraudulent announcement of "improvement" on the morning of the Wisconsin primary election. The jeopardy of the hostages is now worse than ever.

The explanation of this apparent paradox is simple.

Although the Carter administration is directly responsible for the entire Iran crisis, down to the present date, Carter is merely nominally President of the United States. This point has been stressed to leading circles abroad by Henry A. Kissinger on a number of occasions. As Kissinger states accurately enough, Carter is not the President of the United States; the Trilateral Commission is. Henry Kissinger is the prominent "hired gun" for the Trilateral Commission, effectively outranking the puppet Carter in the real ordering of government of the United States.

In brief, insofar as Carter is conducting the Iran policy of the joint-owners of the Trilateral Commission, the New York Council on Foreign Relations, and the Bilderberg cabal, Carter is fully responsible for the Iran situation. However, when Carter has attempted to exploit the Iran situation for a purpose skew to the intent of his masters, Carter discovers repeatedly that his own putative agents, such as Ramsey Clark, take orders from him only to the extent higher authorities instruct them to do so.

Kissinger is correct on one point. Carter is not actually the President of the United States; he is merely the dull tool used by the Trilateral Commission, the object filling up the vacancy which the Constitution specifies as the presidency. That does not mean that the mentally unbalanced Carter is nonexistent; as long as the Trilateraloids act through that dull tool, its idiosyncrasies do delimit and mar the workmanship of which the Trilateral Commission is capable.

Mr. Carter may have his own ideas about exploiting the Iranian hostage situation. His masters have somewhat different intentions.

These samplings of the present situation in the United States suffice to demonstrate that the initial phase of a fascist, totalitarian regime has been introduced under Carter. It makes the complementary, implicit point: What a miserable lot of political sheep most of the citizens of the United States have proven themselves to be in tolerating this aggravated outrage against our nation.

In part, even the "conservative" element of that sheeplike collection has proffered some toleration of Mr. Carter, in response to a perception that Carter might be beginning to "stand up to Moscow!".

2

THE DECLINE OF
THE PATRIOTS

Recently, the former British ambassador to the
United States, Peter Jay, contributed a ten-page review of the political situation in the United States
to the *London Economist*. Jay is a British journalist
whose career has been conspicuously furthered by
his marriage to the daughter of former prime minister and British Labour Party leader James Callaghan. Until the British general election which replaced the Callaghan government with that of
Mrs. Margaret Thatcher, Jay had been assigned
by Callaghan to be British ambassador to Washington, for the purpose of close relations between
Jimmy Carter and the Jay household.

Not only is Jay something of an insider to
British corridors of power—if of low rank—but
the devotion of ten pages of the Round Table's
chief popular organ, the *Economist*, to Jay's rant-
ings, suggests that some special importance was
attached to Jay's piece by much higher ranking
elements.

Reading Jay's article from sentence to sentence, paragraph to paragraph, the piece is chiefly an almost-constant driveling of outright lies and distortions. If one stands back from the pages, so to speak, as if to deemphasize the trees in favor of a view of the forest, some sensible, and important, observations can be made.

In an article which shifts back and forth from the United States to the European Monetary System, Jay presents the following principal points.

In respect to the United States, Jay is alarmed by elements of "volatility" emerging in the primary elections of 1980. Jay's crowd is fully informed that LaRouche received over 20 percent of the votes cast in the February 26 New Hampshire Democratic primary, and is keenly aware LaRouche might have run off with that election but for the most massive "containment" and "dirty tricks" operations. Indeed, London ordered these actions, deployed through such various, cooperating agencies as the Carter administration, the Kennedy campaign, and the morality-free thugs of the Anti-Defamation League. Furthermore, as a curious by-product of the LaRouche New Hampshire campaign, Governor Ronald Reagan began to run away with the Republican nomination. Such developments, centered around LaRouche's "dark horse" campaign, show that the top-down control over the U.S. electorate is being maintained only with wildly felonious measures of a draconian sort by the forces controlling the Carter administration. Hence, the concern over "volatility."

Jay locates the "volatility" in the threatened resurgence of what he terms "American nationalism." If we overlook the Georgetown University crowd's control over Ronald Reagen himself, and focus on the temper of the small avalanche of populist support for Reagan's candidacy, Mr. Jay's point is clear enough empirically. The same sort of observation is to be made for the more than 20 percent of the Democratic vote LaRouche received in New Hampshire, and, since Jay's article, the 12 percent LaRouche received from labor, farmer, black-urban, and other constituencies in Wisconsin.

The causal connection, between the empirics of the LaRouche campaign and Reagan's base of popularity, can be made much more explicit. Reagan carried New Hampshire on the basis of the LaRouche campaign's intensive focus on the fact that the Trilateral Commission controlled both Carter and Republican candidate George Bush. The *Wall Street Journal* broke the story of the connection as a front-page lead story during February. Since then, the *Christian Science Monitor* and spokesmen for the Trilateral Commission itself have been performing public backflips, trying to neutralize the spreading influence of the LaRouche campaign and its various imitators on this point.

To the ordinary American citizen, it appears that the proverbial "everything imaginable" is going wrong. U.S. foreign policy is a spiral of ever-worsening disasters; domestic monetary and economic policy are viewed by the citizen as worse than foreign policy. Clearly, someone is to blame, and that someone must necessarily be an agency of considerable power working from behind the scenes.

The LaRouche campaign's exposure of the Trilateral Commission "caught on" not only because the facts reported are true—LaRouche exposed the Trilateral Commission accurately enough in 1976. It catches on, because a growing portion of the citizenry is searching for the identity of the agency behind the ruin of the United States.

In short, as Peter Jay fears, the United States citizenry, by and large, is potentially ripe for a rebirth of "American nationalism."

Jay gloats as his article summarizes his view of the past forty years of U.S. internal political history. He reports that "American nationalism" was still a ponderable force during the 1930s. However, he continues, under the conditions of the approaching and on-going war, Britain combined forces with the U.S.A.'s "liberal Eastern Establishment" to neutralize the "nationalists," and to establish the Anglo-American alliance's domination over the internal political life of the United States.

In general, Jay's portrait is broadly close to actuality. Whether all "conservative" patriots can free themselves from illusions to agree with this report as I state it, or not, the fact is that the variety of "conservative" typified by the *Spotlight* reader is one of the surviving vestiges of the 1930s "nationalist" faction. In general, Jay is accurate in emphasizing a conspiratorial effort by British-Canadian and liberal Eastern Establishment forces, to isolate and grind that "nationalist" faction down to its present proportions.

What the "nationalist" prefers to deny, often enough, is the fact that it has been his own credulous attitude toward "the Anglo-American anticommunist special partnership," and the control of most of the U.S. intelligence establishment by the tradition of the wartime "Special Operations Executive" arrangement of U.S. intelligence subordination to Britain, which has led most of the "nationalists" to connive in effect at their own undoing.

This brings us to the other principal point of Jay's article, the possible effect of the rise of the European Monetary System in catalyzing an upsurge in American nationalism. Here, Jay's allusion to the LaRouche campaign is properly unmistakable.

Jay observes, somewhat accurately, that the idea of developing supranational institutions for Western Europe had been initially encouraged by Britain. However, Jay laments, the course of the Giscard-Schmidt alliance around the creation of the European Monetary System had worked to an effect directly opposite to British intentions. The European Monetary System is actually strengthening the power and assertiveness of nationalist impulses in economy and political affairs.

The fear Jay emphasizes to his readers is the possibility that the effects of the European Monetary System might spill over into the United States to cause strengthened upsurges of American nationalism.

There has been only one manifestation of a tendency to introduce the European Monetary System as an issue into the U.S. election-process: the LaRouche campaign. That has tended to spill over from the LaRouche campaign into aspects of the Reagan campaign, notably in the form of Congressman Jack Kemp's support for a gold-based dollar, and Kemp's proposal of capital-formation-fostering tax incentives, rather than budget-balancing "fiscal austerity."

Jay's article in the *London Economist* poses several complementary questions to the American nationalist. Two are outstanding. First, by what tricks did the British and liberal Eastern Establishment dupe the nationalist during the postwar years? Second, how do we free ourselves from continued slavery to our ancient enemy, Britain, at this stage—when we have already entered the initial phase of a British-dictated, fascist totalitarian dictatorship?

In partial answer to both questions: On both

counts, we must first free our minds of those delusions which have been employed to enslave us so.

First, What Happened During the War?

On two documented occasions at the outset of World War II, at both the Atlantic and Casablanca meetings with Winston Churchill, President Franklin Roosevelt laid out to an almost-apoplectic Churchill an American doctrine that was, as given, the best statement of American nationalism given up to that point during this century—much better than Roosevelt's opponents among American nationalists at home were offering at that time.

Roosevelt made two interrelated statements of policy. First, never again were the American people to go to war to preserve the British Empire, either in its old form or some new guise. Second, no more was the United States going to tolerate a world run according to "eighteenth century British methods," that is, no longer according to the doctrines associated with Adam Smith. The United States was determined to destroy the last vestiges of the British Empire, and to develop what we today term "the developing sector" with high-technology applications of "American methods."

What became of those resolves? By the time of Roosevelt's death, most of that resolve had already been undone by the like of the cronies of Bernard Baruch in the Roosevelt administration. Bretton

Woods, the "Morgenthau Plan," and related policies had been adopted, strictly according to British interests. All that remained was Roosevelt's agreements with Chiang Kai-Shek, and the agreements of both with Josef Stalin. All but the mask of the "American Century" doctrine for the postwar world was to be wiped aside immediately after Roosevelt's death.

We should have taken India from the British at the end of the war. Not taken it as a colony, but joined forces with Pandit Nehru to make India's "American-style" postwar high-technology development the "jewel" of American global policy. We could have done it; we should have done it.

We should have maintained our alliance with our wartime protégé Ho Chi Minh in Vietnam, the man who wished to become the "George Washington" of his nation, who had been busily copying from the U.S. Declaration of Independence and studying our Constitution to that purpose.

We should have booted Britain out of the Middle East. We should have adopted the nationalist forces associated with Iran's Mohammed Mossadegh, and dictated a peaceful accommodation between Jews and Arabs in Palestine. We should have taken the Jewish refugees from Europe into the United States, rather than letting the British herd them cruelly, by way of such horror-shows as Cyprus concentration camps, into the Middle East.

We let the British, to the mutual astonishment

Alexander Hamilton

Thomas Jefferson

Jefferson was the American proponent of British-controlled Jacobinism. Above, Danton who led the storming of the Bastille (below) on behalf of the British.

of Josef Stalin and Washington, pull their assets on both sides in China to bring Mao Tse-Tung to power. Then, we deluded ourselves that Stalin had done it!

These statements just made are true. To the extent you, the reader, have had contrary beliefs engrained into you over the decades since the late 1940s, the objections you offer to the foregoing statements of fact are samples of the way in which you were duped into aiding your own undoing.

Several things happened during the war. The most obvious subversion was conducted from the British-Canadian side, through what was known as the Special Operations Executive (SOE) of Lord Beaverbrook's Canadian-based crowd around Sir William Stephenson.

In a sense, the SOE never existed, except in the duped eyes of the Americans. It was, as one British intelligence figure recently put the point publicly, a "rib taken out of SIS [Secret Intelligence Services]," to ensure that only those aspects of British intelligence which London chose to expose to the Americans would be placed in view of joint operations. The real operation against the United States was run out of SIS circles overlapping the London Royal Institute of International Affairs, deploying such British spies as Harvard University's William Yandell Elliot, the man who later gave us Henry Kissinger and Zbigniew Brzezinski.

The two principal counterintelligence capabilities of the United States, the Office of Naval Intelligence and "Division V" of the FBI, were British intelligence-"coordinated" during and after the war. The later Rand Corporation, and its wartime predecessor, the U.S. Strategic Bombing Survey, were subsidiaries of the Tavistock Psywar Executive of British intelligence. The element which later became the National Security Agency was also a subdivision of British intelligence.

By hoodwinking the United States with the SOE "dog and pony show," the American intelligence services were kept busy, solving the mazes that British intelligence created and controlled. By taking control of the new eyes and ears the British designed and coordinated as our "new intelligence capability," the British deployed the ability to convince us in "secret" that the sky was orange and the sea pink. Our fascination with "secret" information overrode the plain evidence of our senses.

Many of you know, as do I, of numerous instances in which intelligence-connected people cling obsessively to belief in utter nonsense, simply because they obtained the nonsensical "facts" under cover of a "Q" clearance.

The arrangement works on approximately the same principles as a monkey-trap. "To catchee good-natured, dumb American high-level intelligence operative, place in a narrow-mouthed steel vessel a nut just large enough to be inserted into the opening. Tell dumb American object in vessel is highly secret intelligence. Dumb American will sit with hand around nut, caught in trap, all year long."

The "Cold War" Monkey-Trap

Greece and China were the two leading instances among the operations the British used to securely snare the dumb Americans in what later became known as the "Cold War." The British killed a Truman representative in Greece, blaming it on the Greek Communists, and secured the "Truman Doctrine." The British used a combination of agents inside the Kuomintang to break the Roosevelt-Stalin-Chiang Kai-Shek agreement for postwar China, and used the same facilities to bring Mao Tse-Tung to power in China.

The dumb Americans were convinced that Josef Stalin had "stolen China." Why not? Did not high-level intelligence, conduited from British agents, through British-controlled conduits produce "facts" which proved that, just as the British similarly "proved" that Greek communists had killed the American representative they themselves had ordered wasted?

Volumes of books and corroborating documents existed proving that the Mao Tse-Tung group had been British intelligence "assets" from the beginning. The British caused us to be informed differently, so we ignored all of the evidence in plain sight, just as we ignored the tons of evidence concerning British control of high-level "assets" relevant to the matter within the Kuomintang.

Similarly in Eastern Europe. Not only did Stalin intend to keep strictly to his agreements concerning Eastern Europe, but he had suppressed Eastern European Communist takeovers rather brutally to this purpose. His bloody installation of the Benes government in Czechoslovakia is exemplary. When the British launched their insistent destabilization operations under such covers as UNRRA, Stalin began to react, slowly, ponderously, ruthlessly. By 1948, Stalin operated on purely military-strategic considerations, reducing Eastern Europe to a collection of Soviet military "buffer states," to ensure a military-logistical base for potential Red Army thrusts into Central Europe.

Meanwhile, in a connected policy matter, with the aid of the growing adversary status of Moscow, the British hoodwinked us for a while out of developing nuclear energy.

By 1947, the United States was within reach of developing experimental forms of commercial fission energy plants. Had we continued the Manhattan Project to this purpose, we could never have been vulnerable to British use of the "oil weapon" against us during the past ten years. The Baruch Plan postponed any such undertaking until after it was firmly established that Moscow had developed an operational H-bomb.

Remember the arguments for the Baruch Plan? It was argued that the secrets of nuclear weapons must be kept from the hands of the Soviets.

That was sheer fraud. Prior to the war, Moscow had been significantly ahead of the United States in nuclear technology, having adopted a commitment to development of nuclear energy as early as the mid-1920s under Vladimir Vernadsky. Only economic constraints of the wartime period, not lack of scientific knowledge, prevented the Soviets from developing nuclear weapons under Stalin's Vernadsky-led 1940 "Atom Project." Once we had exploded nuclear weapons, and then ventured into an adversary posture against Moscow, it was certain that Moscow would quickly develop an operational fission weapon.

The "secrecy" arrangement did not hinder Moscow's development of nuclear weapons in the least. In fact, the notion that "atom spies" somehow gave Moscow such capabilities, in whole or part, was a complete hoax.

The significance, the true purpose, of Baruch's activities was made clearer in the instance of Robert Oppenheimer's objections to developing the H-bomb.

The point of the H-bomb is that its development involves an aspect of physics the British wished to suppress: the Riemannian physics of isentropic compression, one of the leading outgrowths of what the British have combatted for centuries as "continental science." We had this sort of physics through, inclusively, figures such as Dr. Edward Teller, who had the benefits of the Riemannian-centered physics tradition of Germany's Göttingen University. The leading edge of Russian physics, since the Petrograd, Leibniz-Euler based tradition of pre-Bolshevik times, was a very advanced complement to the Göttingen physics tradition. That was the physics which made Penemunde a success, a fact which both the United States and Moscow had not overlooked in acquiring German specialists at the close of the war.

The Britishers' anticontinental science ideology got the better of them. The coincidence in Soviet and U.S. development of the H-bomb proved that anglophile Oppenheimer's arguing for the British policy was lunatic, as well as simply wrong.

Soviet development of the H-bomb killed off plans for a "preventive" nuclear war against Moscow during the late 1950s. We dumped Senator Joseph McCarthy, because his usefulness had been outlived by the Soviet H-bomb, and because he also became too big for his britches in tampering with the military. The more self-controlled warriors, such as Senator Hubert Humphrey, adapted quite nicely to the shift from "McCarthyism" to "Cold War."

It was these and other means used by the British to develop the postwar adversary relationship between Moscow and Washington which achieved the most in keeping the United States under British control. This ruined America's patriotic nationalists as a political force, by obliging them to refrain from even suspecting an adversary relationship in fact to our "staunch anticommunist ally" Great Britain.

A similar development occurred on Moscow's side. "The American Imperialist Adversary" became the touchstone of Soviet policy-making, just as the "Soviet enemy" became the axiomatic basis for every aspect of U.S. foreign policy, and much of domestic policy as well.

There was, and is a "communist" problem, but the reality of that problem is skew by comparison with the popularized assumptions dominating U.S. opinion since the late 1940s. Let us leave the aspect of the matter we have been reviewing so far, and return to it after we have now, next examined the real "communist" danger.

3

WHAT IS 'COMMUNISM'?

The Communist Party U.S.A. is right on one, and perhaps only one point: the first, true leading communist in the United States was Thomas Jefferson, atheism and all.

The essentials of the Jefferson story are summarized by Donald Phau in the March 1980 issue of *The Campaigner*, so we need not repeat that account in detail here. We refer to those matters only as they are essential reference for the points on which we are focused here.

The true origins of the modern communist movement in general are located in what the Marquis de Lafayette identified to Washington as the Jesuit creation of the Jacobins deployed by the British government against France during the 1789-1794 period, the Jacobins of Jesuit-Hospitaller "asset" Robespierre, and of British agents Danton and Marat.

During the 1830s, British intelligence, largely under direction of Lord Palmerston, created two complementary movements. One was the "Oxford

fundamentalist" movement, a "charismatic" gnos-
tic-modeled cult based on the practices of the
ancient cults of Apollo and Isis. The other was the
"neo-Jacobin" movement, of which the "Young
America" Transcendentalists of Concord and Harvard were a part, and which spawned a variety of
radical, anticapitalist organizations in Europe.
Among these were the "Chartists" and the Communist League. The exemplar outgrowths of this
neo-Jacobinism included the founders of the
anarchist movement, Proudhon, Stirner, and
Bakunin.

We shall turn to the problem of pseudo-Christian "charismatic" cults in an ensuing chapter.
Now, we shall focus on both the British-created
"communist" movement generally, and also the
particular, paradoxical position of Karl Marx as
a one-time "asset" of the British intelligence
service.

The point respecting Jefferson is that he was
wittingly complicit with British intelligence in operations against the United States, and that he was
the leader of the British intelligence effort to
spread the Jacobin movement into the United
States as a battering ram against the forces, headed
by Franklin, Washington, and Hamilton, dedicated to creating the first capitalist constitutional
republic.

Jefferson's correspondence with Jeremy Bentham and other leading figures of British intelli-

gence proves that he was wittingly, not coincidentally, committed to the cause of Britain in those various Jacobin and other actions he took to weaken the young United States. This aids us in evaluating the significance of the work of undercover agents of the British intelligence service in promoting Jefferson—against Washington, Hamilton, et al. as the idol of certain strata of duped conservatives.

The key to Jefferson's link to British-made communism is also symptomized in an important way by his position as the highest-ranking proponent of Adam Smith's anti-American *Wealth of Nations* inside the United States. It was Jefferson who led in promoting the destruction of the National Bank of the United States, in eliminating a central command for U.S. military defenses, in almost destroying the naval and army forces developed to a high quality of fighting force by Washington and Inspector-General Alexander Hamilton. It was Jefferson who protected the treasonous "New England Secessionists," and who conducted a zealous rearguard action in the effort to delay Burr's indictment for treason, and to aid in preventing Burr's conviction on that charge.

As we shall see, it was Jefferson's support for the anticapitalist doctrine of Adam Smith which is key to such aspects of Jefferson's role in nearly effecting our conquest by Britain during the course of the War of 1812.

That is the significance of British agents' duping many American conservatives into adopting the fraudulent faith that Adam Smith's doctrine of "free trade" is the wellspring of the United States' former economic greatness.

Adam Smith: Communist

Adam Smith was a propaganda agent for both the British East India Company and the Edinburgh-centered division of the British Secret Intelligence Service. In that latter connection, he was the immediate subordinate and continuing collaborator of David Hume, including his collaboration with Hume in the creation of that synthetic cult, the "Ossian" cult, out of which the Odin and Thule cults of Hitler's Nazis were directly derived via the Wittelsbach (Bavaria) and Hapsburg (Vienna) court circles. (It was the Thule Society, that gave the Nazis their cult symbol, the swastika.)

In addition to being a fraud and a liar, Smith was generally a nasty fellow.

There was no contradiction between Smith's dual services to SIS and the East India Company.

The modern capitalist republic is in a direct, and essentially intended outgrowth of the work of an Augustinian current which the British rather frequently denounce as the "Raphaelites." (Hence, John Ruskin's association with the self-styled "pre-Raphaelites," the feudalists dedicated to undoing the changes in European culture effected by the

Raphaelites.) This Raphaelite current is associated with the White Guelph opponents of the Black Guelph faction of the turn of the fourteenth century, and with the leading political figure for the White Guelphs, Dante Alighieri.

To situate this summarily, the following background facts should be added.

Dante's predecessors include the Holy Roman Emperors in the tradition of Alcuin and Charlemagne, including the Salier and Staufer houses generally. These currents were a direct outgrowth of the Neoplatonic Christianity of the Apostles and of such patristics as Saint Augustine. This matter we shall examine more closely as we take up the issue of pseudo-Christian, cultist "Oxford fundamentalism." However, despite the technological progress effected under such Augustinian "city-builders," the attempt to establish a republic of Christendom was shown to be a political error.

The principal difficulty was that the establishment of a pan-European Christendom depended upon a *lingua franca*, specifically Latin. This left the ordinary people with a brutish form of illiterate speech, the demotic languages and dialects of Europe. Under this arrangement it was impossible to lift a majority of the population into a condition of citizenship. The brutalized masses of the rural population became, repeatedly, the crazed rabbles used by the enemies to destroy the republican order.

Therefore, as we note in connection with Dante's work on the potential eloquence of the Italian language, it was discovered to be essential to educate the spoken demotic languages of Europe as written languages capable of communicating conceptions above the level of beastlike peasant gruntings, meanwhile absorbing groups of dialects and obscure languages into a common, educated, literate demotic language.

The kind of political ordering this required was analyzed in Dante's *De Monarchia*. The internal geometry of three distinct species of judgment and morality was rigorously examined in Dante's most famous writing, his *Commedia*.

Dante was, like Apostolic Christianity itself, "Neoplatonic." This underlines the significance of Raphael's "The Academy of Athens" as a political work of that period, and accounts for the British hatred of Raphael.

These new proposals, associated with Dante et al., appeared in the midst of one of the worst horrors the Christian era has witnessed, the "new dark age," which ranged over the period from the overthrow of the Staufer through the conclusion of the Black Death. Over this period, the population of Europe was halved by interconnected famine, epidemic, and social chaos—half the parishes of Europe disappeared so. That genocidal "new dark age," with its associated outbursts of "charismatic," pseudo-Christian cults (such as the flagellants), was the direct consequence of the "zero technological growth" policies of the Black Guelph, combined with the "fiscal austerity" of those Black Guelph bankers, such as the Bardi and Perruzi, who seized control of the monarchical and other feudal debts of that period.

It was in such circumstances of the late fourteenth century that the conspiratorial forces of Dante's direct successors worked to the purpose or eradicating forever the sort of policies brought upon Europe by the Isis-cultist "black nobility" families of Italy.

For sake of brevity here, one efficiently grasps the connection of the fifteenth-century Neoplatonic republicans to Dante's circles by comparing the works of the leading figures of the first half of the fifteenth century, Cardinal Nicholas of Cusa and Plethon, with the cited works of Dante Alighieri.

During the fifteenth century, the rentier-financial power of the black nobility, the ancient Roman senatorial families of Isis cultists, was centered in the Genoese bankers. These forces, the combined forces of the Roman senatorial families and the Genoese, turned Byzantium over to their protégé the Turkish conqueror—supplying the Turkish forces with cannon for this enterprise, with the Genoese opening the gates of Constantinople. They also took over control of Spain under Ferdinand and Isabella, bringing a Guelph feudal

family, the Hapsburgs, to power in Spain. With
the aid of the Hapsburgs and the use of Spanish
puppets' military forces, the black nobility wrecked
the power of the republicans in most of Italy itself,
concluding their success with the death of Cesare
Borgia.

However, the republicans also had their suc-
cesses. Their first success was the establishment of
the first modern nation-state, France, under Louis
XI. Louis XI's success created the strategic environment which weakened the black nobility forces
in England—but not Scotland—sufficiently to permit the establishment of the second modern nation-state under Henry VII of Tudor England.

It was through those two republican revolutions
of the late fifteenth century, in France and England, that the European nation-state was established as an institution. Republican capitalism is
the direct outgrowth of the explicit policies of
Louis XI and the early Tudors.

During the sixteenth century, the republican
forces were organized as the "commonwealth"
parties of England and France. This was the origin
of the seventeenth-century Commonwealth Party
of England, the founder of most of the American
English-speaking colonies. That party was more
commonly known as *Les Politiques* in France, the
party of the House of Navarre, and of Tremblay,
as well as Richelieu, Mazarin, and Jean-Baptiste
Colbert. This was the faction allied with Cromwell

against the Hapsburgs and Stuart, and was responsible for establishing French settlements (as opposed to Jesuit fur-trading operations) in North America. The object of those seventeenth-century colonies in North America was to create on these shores republics which, becoming strengthened, would tip the strategic balance of power decisively against the feudalist factions of Europe.

The United States was not a product of "misunderstandings" with Britain erupting during the late eighteenth century; the object of establishing such a republic on these shores had been proposed by, among others, Robert Dudley, during the sixteenth century, before the first English colonization was attempted.

During the last half of the sixteenth century, spearheaded by the combined forces of the Genoese and their principal secret intelligence operation, the Jesuits, England was reconquered by the black nobility, and the House of Orange corrupted into becoming a leading Protestant cover for the Jesuit order. This conquest of England was aided by the Genoese puppet-state of Scotland, and implemented through the most evil family of Britain—down to the present date—the Cecils.

Beginning 1589, and culminating in the 1603 accession of James I to the newly created throne of the United Kingdom, the Jesuit-Genoese agents, the Cecils, together with the Jesuit Cecil relative, Francis Bacon, conducted a blood-purge of leading ranks of the Commonwealth Party and the British Secret Intelligence Service, ridding themselves of such English agents of SIS as the real "007," John Dee, and also such SIS operatives as Shakespeare's mentor, Christopher Marlowe.

What James I did to the capitalist development of England, with aid of Francis Bacon, the embezzling Chancellor of the Exchequer, exemplifies the real issue between Adam Smith and Alexander Hamilton, between American System capitalism and the communism of Thomas Jefferson. James looted England by placing its national debt under the control of foreign tax-farmers, while tearing down the system of regulation that protected and nourished the capitalist industry developed during the sixteenth century.

The Commonwealth Party's victories in seventeenth-century England paralleled the victories of the *politiques* under Mazarin and Mazarin's successor, Colbert, in France. The reconquest of England by forces led by the Genoese-allied House of Orange, first putting the Stuarts back on the throne, transferred the bastion of the English-speaking section of the Commonwealth Party from England to the Commonwealth colonies in North America.

The British East India Company, the author of the policy which obliged the Americans to fight against Britain, was the principal outgrowth of the system of Genoese tax-farming first imposed upon

England by James I in 1603, and restored to power in 1660.

As Henry and Mathew Carey and Friedrich List, among others, emphasized during the first half of the nineteenth century, the British political economic system defended by the French Physiocrats, and by Smith, Thomas Malthus, David Ricardo, and John Stuart Mill, is not a capitalist form of political economy. It is a mixture of capitalist forms of industrial development with ruling feudal elements. It is capitalism subordinated to a feudalist rentier system, or what is generically termed "monetarism" today.

The British political economic system, ruling by a tiny proportion of the whole population, depends upon periodic deploying of hordes of rural and urban anticapitalist rabble, such as the French Jacobins, to so weaken the capitalist republican faction of industry and labor that the feudalist rule remains effectively unchallenged. That combination of rural and urban anticapitalist rabble is "communism."

The *Wealth of Nations* of Adam Smith is both an apology for the rentier system of British feudalism, and a lying attack on the political economy of capitalist republicanism, the capitalist republicanism developed as a systematic doctrine first by the combined work of France's Jean-Baptiste Colbert and Colbert's protégé Gottfried Wilhelm Leibniz. The American System, as articulated at the outset of the federal republic by Washington's Treasury Secretary Alexander Hamilton, in connection with *credit, banking,* and *manufactures,* is the direct expansion of the policies articulated by Colbert and Leibniz.

The policies of Adam Smith are the policies against which the American Revolution was fought. Never has Adam Smith been acquainted with capitalist republicanism in the United States, except by traitors and dupes. Jefferson was such a traitor.

Jefferson was: (1) self-defined as a British agent-of-influence against the United States federal republic through his correspondence and his related, witting role in introducing Jacobinism into the United States; (2) a feudalist, not only because of his plantation interests, and his view of negroes as subhuman creatures to be treated humanely, but because of his physiocratic delusions, his advocacy of Adam Smith, and his adoption of the feudalist doctrines of Jean-Jacques Rousseau and Jeremy Bentham's hedonism; (3) a "communist" in the strict sense, because of the witting Benthamism of his Jacobinism.

As numerous among "conservatives" must recognize, the cult of "libertarian Jefferson" is a most prominent feature of the penetration of communist ideological influences to the effect of promoting "conservative libertarianism" in their ranks.

"Communism," again, is the deployment of

anticapitalist rabble, such as the "Naderite environmentalists," together with doctrines of "free trade," to wreck both high-technology capital formation and the essentially "dirigist" institutions of *credit, banking*, and *protectionism* of technologically progressive enterprise which are the essential institutions of a capitalist republic in general, and the American System of Hamilton, the Careys, List, and Abraham Lincoln most emphatically.

4

KARL MARX'S COMMUNISM

Modern communism, taken as a whole, is the direct outgrowth of anarchoid neo-Jacobin movements set into motion by British intelligence during the 1830s, and as a complement, as we have already noted, to the irrationalist cultism launched during the same period, "Oxford fundamentalism."

The immediate reason for that 1830s promotion of "neo-Jacobinism" by such leading British responsibles as Lord Palmerston was the revival of the influence of the American System under U.S. Presidents Monroe and John Quincy Adams, and the aid to the cause of the United States and the spread of the American System by the head of U.S. foreign intelligence during that period, the leader of the international Cincinnatus Society, the Marquis de Lafayette.

The feudalist world-order which the British and their Hapsburg-centered allies thought to have secured through the wrecking actions of Jefferson,

Madison, and the 1815 Treaty of Vienna was freshly threatened.

From 1789 to 1815

Despite the near-wrecking of France's republican potentialities by the Jacobin episode, the Thermidorians around Lazare Carnot and his collaborator Gaspard Monge built a republican force around the centerpiece of the Ecole Polytechnique. In addition to promoting the industrial-technological progress of France and Germany, and despite Napoleon's follies, the circles around Carnot had created the republican military system, had fostered a quantum-leap in science in the tradition of Leibniz, and had produced scientific advances over Hamilton's statement of the American System, notably through such associates of the Carnot-Monge circle as François Ferrier, Claude Chaptal, and Charles Dupin.

But for Napoleon, chiefly Napoleon's estrangement of the German republicans, the American System would have prevailed throughout most of European culture during the first quarter of the nineteenth century. Thus, the wrecking of the United States's economy through the administrations of Jefferson and Madison, and the feudal order superimposed on Europe by the 1815 Treaty of Vienna, assured the British and Hapsburgs that the menace of the American System had been effectively corked up.

From about 1818 onwards, the menace became considerably uncorked. At about that time, Nicholas Biddle's Second Bank of the United States was made effective, British "free trade" policies were repudiated, in favor of a return to the American System, and West Point was upgraded as a center of engineering as well as military training, on the basis of the Carnot model.

It was during this same period that Lafayette came back into prominence, nearly succeeding in his last conspiratorial venture, the aborted efforts of 1830.

Meanwhile, prior to 1830, Lafayette integrated the alliance of his European republican circles to the American Whigs. His extended tour of the United States in 1824 was crucial. He concluded his tour by bringing into the United States a brilliant German republican, Friedrich List, a student of the work of the French economists Ferrier, Chaptal, and Dupin, as well as the work of Hamilton.

List was integrated into the Philadelphia-centered headquarters of the U.S. intelligence service, around the publishing house of a close collaborator of both Benjamin Franklin and Alexander Hamilton, Mathew Carey. List was assigned to organize among German-Americans in the vicinity of Reading—where he edited the Reading *Adler*, a direct predecessor to today's Reading *Eagle*. Otherwise, List emerged as the leading economist of the American System. After taking U.S. citizenship in 1830, List departed immediately for Europe, to join Lafayette's efforts of that immediate period.

List, working in close collaboration with the publisher von Cotta, the leading German connection for Lafayette during that period, emerged as the key figure in refining and implementing von Cotta's on-going project, the creation of the German "customs union."

Britain's alarm at these and related developments was reflected in a crucial way in the attack on the decayed condition of British science by Charles Babbage and others of the Edinburgh-Cambridge faction of that period. The United States, France, Germany, and Russia had leaped so far ahead of Britain in the fundamentals of science that only one person in all Britain could be found capable of reporting the principal features of new European continental developments in mathematical physics.

Under the influence of the circles associated with von Cotta and List, Germany was projecting the development of railways as the key to an industrial infrastructure. The metals industry of the Ruhr was organized as a sophisticated, dirigist conspiracy, as was the chemical industry.

If European republicanism could succeed in mobilizing a growing popular base for science and American System approaches to economic development, France and Germany, combined with the United States itself, would soon make the American System hegemonic, a force a self-weakened Britain could not efficiently counter.

British Philosophical Radicalism

During the last decades of the eighteenth century, the lessons of Britain's defeat by the transatlantic republicans in the American Revolution had been reflected in the rise of the new regime of Lord Shelburne, and Shelburne's key protégés, William Pitt the Younger and Jeremy Bentham. This was otherwise a political dictatorship of Britain created by agreement of George III with the immediate sponsorship of the East India Company and Barings Bank.

Although Bentham and James Mill's essential outlook was not different from that of Locke and Hume, the distinction of Bentham's work was to elaborate Hume's immoral "indifferentism," or "empiricism," as a body of foul social practice. This body of social practice Bentham entitled "hedonism." This amounted to the systematic promotion of pederasty, "radical feminism" (for example, Mary Wollstonecraft Shelley), "recreational" drug use, (for example, Coleridge et al.), and various pseudo-Christian and overtly Satanist cults, as tactics for degrading strata of the population into the state Dante analyzes in the "Inferno" canticle of his *Commedia*.

Bentham was otherwise a raving fascist, to whom the Nazi concentration camps and "useless eaters" slave-labor policies owe their inspiration. His *Panopticon* scheme is the direct precedent for the Nazi concentration camps; his labor policies are the precedent for the Nazi policy of using up "useless eaters" through labor-intensive servitude.

That was the character of this key influence on the world-outlook of Thomas Jefferson.

This was the basis for the genocidal policies of a lower-ranking servant of the British East India Company, Thomas Malthus, a typical British Anglican parson in his ethical makeup.

During the 1820s and 1830s, the nominally Protestant Jesuit families of Britain (for example, the Cecil-centered grouping) reformulated Bentham's hedonism as what became known to initiates thereafter as "British philosophical radicalism," the essential doctrine of William F. Buckley and the East Side Conservative Club today; the modern parody of a British "Hells-Fire Club" from the Georgian and Regency periods. In the tenor of the Victorian mode of double-talk, Bentham's hedonism was popularized afresh as the "utilitarianism" of John Stuart Mill et al.

Appropriately, L.D. Trotsky, in his autobiography, praises the influence over himself exerted by Jeremy Bentham. "Hedonism," "utilitarianism," and "radical, atheist materialism" are all the same matter.

By creating the "radical republican nationalists" of the 1830s and 1840s, the British seduced the youth of the Lafayette-centered republican families into neutralization, to a large degree, of the capitalist republicanism of their fathers.

This reminds us, properly, of the doctrine of the ancient subcult of the cult of Apollo, the Phrygian cult of Dionysus. The cult of Dionysus seduced the young from the leading families of the republican cities, using pornography, "sexual freedom" plus pederasty, intoxication and "disco"-like dance orgies, as part of the "brainwashing" procedure by which these youth were deployed as assassins against their fathers. That ancient model for modern, Jesuit-initiated international terrorism of today, was an instrument, then as now, of the antirepublican oligarchists against the urban-centered republican forces of scientific and technological progress.

Barry Commoner and Ralph Nader are not peculiar to the modern age. They are an evil as old as sin itself in the recorded annals of history. They are, in modern terms of reference, expressions of the archetypical communists created by combined efforts of the Jesuits and British intelligence.

Enter Karl Marx

Noting Heinrich Marx's regretable softness toward Rousseau, Karl Marx is exemplary of those children of early nineteenth-century, pro-American republicans who were seduced into the cause of British philosophical radicalism over the course of the 1830s and 1840s.

Karl Marx's birthplace, Trier, had been one of the late eighteenth-century "hotbeds" of Franklin's networks of support in the Germany of Leibniz. The director of Marx's gymnasium, Johann Hugo Wyttenbach, had been appointed to that position during the 1790s on grounds of his outstanding position as a representative of the conceptions of Benjamin Franklin and Immanuel Kant. This influence on the young Marx is exhibited most emphatically in an essay (*"Aufsatz"*) written for Wyttenbach's class in 1835. Comparing Marx's essay with those of other students in the same class of 1835, the Neoplatonic republican influence is indisputable.

At what had been Ludwig van Beethoven's university of reference, the republican University of Bonn, Marx assimilated more beer and schnapps than republicanism, according to the tenor of father-son correspondence, and proceeded to Berlin, where he fell, first, under the influence of the Jesuit-influenced "delphic" hoaxster, G. W. F. Hegel, and then under that of the radical "left Hegelians."

However, even then, young Marx's republican impulses had been only corrupted, not destroyed. His appointment, defeating that of candidate Friedrich List, to the editorship of the *Rheinische Zeitung,* shows that he was chosen as less offensive to the British and their German dupes, at that moment, than List, but was otherwise a qualified republican in the eyes of the relevant procapitalist nationalists involved in the enterprise.

During the 1844-1848 period, Marx came increasingly under the subversive influences of Jesuit and British radical circles in Paris, Brussels, and so forth. A careful epistemological evaluation of the characteristics of Marx's writings over the period 1844-1848 reflects the process of corruption underway. The other prominent correlative of this degradation was Marx's qualified break with the Lafayette-faithful republican, Heinrich Heine, toward the close of this interval.

The conflicting tendencies, Marx's weakened Neoplatonic heritage from Trier and his growing adaptation to British philosophical radicalism, reach a turning-point in two key documents from the 1845 period. His "Theses on Feuerbach," and the "Feuerbach" section of the Marx-Engels *The German Ideology* represent Marx at the highest point of intellectual maturity and intellectual accomplishment. Although he never repudiated the essential features of his thought from that period, the positive element in Marx became increasingly contained and dominated by an avalanche of British radical ideology.

It was during this interval that Marx became, unwittingly, an "asset" of the British Secret Intelligence Service. The key figure in this corruption was Friedrich Engels, a witting agent of the Cambridge Apostles' circle of SIS, as well as a scion of a British family whose prosperity was based on black-chattel-slave production of cotton in the United States. The crucial development in making Marx an "asset" of SIS was Engels's success in inducing Marx to write a fraudulent diatribe against Friedrich List, as well as inducing Marx to join Engels in denouncing those who exposed the Rothschilds' hand (such as Rothschild intimate Heinrich Heine) behind the radical-republican ferment of 1844-1848.

There are two aspects to Engels's growing influence over Marx during that period.

First, Marx's hostility to the mainstream, anarchist currents of British-Jesuit communism, such as that of Proudhon, Stirner, and later Bakunin, was clearly intended, in part, by the British. This amounted to a typically Jesuit "delphic" trick, of creating a variety of "communist" packages, so as to appeal more efficiently to the varied susceptibilities among a broader, targeted population. Marx, an established figure among the rational section of the German radicals, served to aid the British in producing a "rational" variety of communism, aimed at the susceptibilities of those who abhorred the pornographic obscenity of the existentialist, anarchist utopians, such as Bakunin and his friend Richard Wagner.

Second, the very qualities of Marx that made

him useful to the British on the first count caused him to become not only problematical, but counted as a "potential danger" to British interests.

This has been a recurring problem for the Jesuit and British controllers of communist movements. Marx and Lenin are exemplary of this. The rational element which a Neoplatonic youth carries into the nightmare lunacy of the communist strata becomes a constant cause of deepening conflict between the rational impulses of that youth and the hedonistic, irrationalist lunacy of British-style communist radicalism. Even Trotsky, who persisted as an avowed Benthamite in heritage after his dislodgement from power, was a mass of philosophical contradictions, on account of the conflict between his Benthamite anarchoid qualities—his engrained anarchosyndicalism—and that desire to cultivate orderly intellectual powers which drew him into the proscience, pro-industrialist currents in the Soviet Union of the 1920s.

In Marx, this conflict took the form of his orientation toward establishing a republican form of industrial society within the context of his socialism. Similarly, Lenin.

This spilled over into practice. In Marx's case, in his support for Abraham Lincoln's defense of the United States as a capitalist republic—an occasion on which the Neoplatonic republican impulses of the young Marx overrode the radicalism of the post-1845 Marx. Lenin's revival of the capitalist entente policy of Czarist minister Count Sergei Witte, in the form of the 1922 Rapallo proposal, is another instance of the same ironies.

There is no competent doubt of the essential conflict between Marx's Neoplatonic impulses and Engels's British radicalism. If one compares the fragment of Engels's aborted draft of the "Feuerbach" section of *The German Ideology* with Marx's substitute, and with Marx's "Theses on Feuerbach," the fundamental differences are clear. Marx attacks Feuerbach for degenerating from Neoplatonic conceptions of Christianity into what was in fact Isis-cultism—in Feuerbach's *The Essence of Christianity*, the substitute of the consubstantial Trinity, which Feuerbach outlines at the beginning of that work, by the Isis-cult model of the "Holy Family." Engels focuses his attack against the Neoplatonic facet of Feuerbach's work.

That is affirmed in Engels's later writings, including his writing on "Ludwig Feuerbach," and his mixture of rabid Benthamism with Huxley-Darwin reductionism in his writings on the family and his posthumously published *Dialectics of Nature*.

Although Engels became attached to his victim, Marx, over the decades of their combined actual and purely nominal associations, that is a source of Engels's psychological complications, not a key to the essential character of his relationship to Marx.

During Marx's period of abject poverty in London, Engels for extended periods never gave Marx more than a pittance of financial assistance, begging prudence as reason for his stinginess, all the while he was himself living in luxury with his succession of mistresses, all on the profits tied to chattel-slavery in the United States. Engels stands out as a creature of despicable unwholesomeness overall.

In London, immediate control over SIS "asset" Marx passed from Engels to David Urquhart of the British Museum. Marx lived in poverty because his British patrons were a stingy lot of parasites, and because the events of 1848-1851 in Germany had reduced Marx's practical importance to them for that time. However, as much patronage as Marx did enjoy from his British hosts was coordinated through Urquhart.

If one searches outside the literature directly pertaining to Marx himself, Urquhart's role for British intelligence stands out clearly, consequently informing us of the precise position he had to Marx during the period of their association.

The British Museum, always a key institution for British intelligence, was the conduit, among other matters, for Palmerston's supervision of the European radicals (whereas Edinburgh was the principal control-center for managing United States assets of British intelligence, such as the Boston-Concord gang). If one wishes today to collect materials on the 1830s-1850s European radical movement, it is to the files associated with Urquhart that one turns for most of the material readily available. The Communist League was one such Palmerston creation, as were the German radicals generally. In the organization of British intelligence at that time, "asset" Karl Marx fell indisputably under the control of Urquhart.

Fitting that broader knowledge of the matter to direct knowledge of the crucial features of part of the Marx-Urquhart connection, little is left to the imagination.

The case of Dr. Edward Aveling illustrates the nature of the actual arrangements around Marx at the British Museum. Aveling, the lover of Annie Besant (of the Theosophy Society, British intelligence's joint anthroposophical project, in cooperation with the Jesuits), seduced Marx's most talented daughter in the British Museum, later driving her to her death after creating a series of international scandals around Marx's name through use of that connection. It was Aveling who attempted to bring Marx into the camp of Darwinism, and Engels who defended Aveling's actions and projects until the appearances no longer permitted the maintenance of such fraud on Engels's part.

Marx's support for Abraham Lincoln was almost the end of British intelligence's toleration of its "asset" Marx. Except for Marx's marginal value to the British on the Russian issue, he was clearly more a net liability than an asset, and was handled accordingly.

Marx as a Political Economist

Marx's position as a political economist is a mixed affair. He clearly did salvage David Ricardo's accounting system, and improved it by the central position Marx gave in that work to an acknowledged debt to List for the notion of "labor-power." Insofar as one can take momentarily at face value the untenable assumption that the British System represents capitalism, Marx's examination of the "fundamental internal contradictions" of the British System are an accurate analytical description, although unsound in respect of the fundamentals of an actual economic process.

In consequence of those two accomplishments, Marx's analysis of the business cycle and of implicit breakdown phenomena conforms significantly to empirical realities insofar as the British System of political economy is imposed upon national economies, or upon world commerce and finance more generally. Thus, Marx as a political economist has gained an appearance of scientific superiority which would be recognized as unjustified wherever an actually scientific economics were known.

Otherwise, Marx's *Capital* and *Theories of Surplus Value* are permeated with a mixture of witting and naive frauds.

The principal deliberate fraud in Marx's political-economic writings is his plagiarism of "labor-power" from Friedrich List. Engels, who had adopted British instructions to deploy into Germany against List, compounds this by lying in crediting Marx with the discovery of "labor-power."

The origin of that conception is the political-economic writings of Leibniz in the seventeenth century. It next appears prominently in the proof given by Alexander Hamilton as the central feature of his 1791 *Report to the Congress on the Subject of Manufactures.* In fact, Hamilton's conception is an order of magnitude more profound than Marx's use of "labor-power." Hamilton defines the use of science and capital-formation ("artificial labor") to increase "the productive powers of labor" as the only possible source of wealth. Marx degrades technological progress to an almost accidental feature of capitalism, following the British perversion on this point.

Although Charles Dupin was the leading French economist of Marx's lifetime, Marx includes no reference to List, Dupin, Chaptal, Ferrier, Hamilton, or Leibniz in his treatment. Marx selects only the feudalist political economists who succeeded William Petty, such as the French Physiocrats, Smith, Malthus, Ricardo, and so forth.

In a similar way, we find in Marx's history of science a fraudulent syncretic blending of Hegel's frauds and British doctrine. Bacon, Hobbes,

Locke, Hume, and so forth are the Engels-dis-
oriented Marx's succession of "progress" in the
development of "scientific materialism."

Yet, despite those mixed witting and naive
frauds in Marx's writings, the contrary impulse of
Neoplatonism breaks through. It does not break
Marx from the "controlled environment" of British frauds in point of historical fact. Rather, it
impels him to transform the British world-view
into a curious miscegenation of Platonism, altering
somewhat a predominantly Aristotelian-reduction-
ist schema consistent with British radical frauds.

This is most efficiently identified as a moment
of paradox within Marx's political economy by
comparing the opening paragraphs of his "Feuerbach" contribution to *The German Ideology* of
1845 with the concluding section VII of *Capital*
III, especially the treatment of "Freedom and
Necessity." In those locations, he defines his
method of creative insight to be Neoplatonic.

Marx has adopted the radicalism of Dante's
"Inferno" as the universe in which he has adopted
a restive sort of citizenship. In that setting, without
perceiving that Hell is Hell, he proposes to reform
Hell with the aid of a fragile glimmer of the
method of "Paradise."

Otherwise, concerning the systematic errors of
Marx's political economy, I first developed the
proverbial last word on that back in 1952, in
employing Riemannian physics to treat the system-

atic error of *Capital* as a whole, thus using Ricardo's accounting categories and Riemannian physics to premise mathematical approaches to economic analysis on Hamilton's elaboration of the notion of the "productive powers of labor."

The actual political-economic thought of Karl Marx, as distinct from the fraudulent representations radiating from Kings College and the London School of Economics, is significant today only insofar as it influences the policies of professedly Marxist nations such as the Soviet Union.

The Case of V.I. Lenin
The case of V.I. Lenin is immediately comparable to that of Karl Marx as we have outlined it above.

In direct opposition to his executed, terrorist brother, young Lenin was essentially Neoplatonic in characteristic features of his outlook. This is exemplified for empirical studies by examining his persistent adoption of the Russian Neoplatonic voluntarist Tchernyshevski as the model of his essential world-outlook, while adopting a somewhat-muddled appreciation of Marx's work, together with the Russian "left," as the appropriated instruments for implementing Tchernyshevskian objectives.

Today, to adduce an accurate perception of the underlying driving tendencies within Soviet Russia one errs unless one sees Leninist development of Russia as a resumption of the rapid industrial and scientific development earlier in progress, from the freeing of the serfs until the British-orchestrated destabilization of the government of Count Sergei Witte at the beginning of this century.

The reader should not delude himself by insisting that the point just made is at best some debatable sort of interpretation of the matter. The point just made is crucial to the formulation of a competent sort of strategic posture toward Moscow today. The point just made may offend engrained convictions, but truth usually does—just as all important discovery must overcome established errors of prevailing assumptions.

At this point, for the sake of the reader, we interpolate here an extremely important bit of methodological counsel.

People act generally under the impulse of two, frequently contradictory kinds of motivation. On the lower level of their natures, people are usually dominated in their decisions and actions by impulses expressing prejudices. Yet, often, the characteristic impulses of their judgment, reflecting a deeper (and higher) aspect of their mental being, are contrary to the implications of specific, consciously adopted beliefs.

Applying this to Moscow, we have the following. In some respects, on the lower, more short-term side, Moscow's policy is shaped by the attempt to bring into practice actions which celebrate belief in this or that point of adopted, "official" Marxist-Leninist doctrine. Yet, apart from such matters of doctrinal persuasion, Soviet leading circles are committed to increasing the productive powers of Soviet labor, and to fostering science, technology, and capital-formation to that end. The impulses arising from the experienced interaction of reality with those latter imperatives often stand in opposition to the deductive applications of Marxist-Leninist doctrine.

There are analogies for this in the realm of physics. In examining inorganic, simple processes, one adduces special, adduced principles of action for that microcosmical aspect of reality. These adductions become doctrinal belief, usually drilled into the retentive powers of helpless students in universities. Yet, the reductionist methods of analysis which have seemed adequate for treating such relatively microcosmical phenomena are not in fact the way even the "inorganic" domain as a whole is actually ordered. So, continued, empirically based progress in the ordinary employment of scientific method of a reductionist sort leads research to the point of what is sometimes termed, variously a "unique" or "crucial" experiment. Such experiments involve a partial or sweeping revolution in the assumptions associated with physics-practice in general. Reality, which does not conform to doctrine, has in that efficient way intruded to overrule previous doctrine.

Such a series of crucial-experimental changes in

the ruling doctrines of taught physics can be—and ought to be treated as empirical phenomena of a special sort. Instead of examining empirical relations among mere objects, let us examine the relations defined as empirical knowledge by the succession of crucial-experimental revolutions in scientific doctrine.

If the doctrines in currency at any point in that arrangement of successive crucial-experimental breakthroughs were taken as absolute, then the entire universe might be assumed to function under the rule of such implied principles of action. Yet, the recurring appearance of the crucial-experimental breakthroughs informs anyone with his or her wits about them, that the assumptions of the naive, reductionist sort of doctrinaire scientists are false with respect to the way in which the universe is actually organized. It is the principle common to the ordered succession of crucial-experimental breakthroughs which appropriately reflects the actual lawful ordering of the universe. If society is to be able to survive the crucial breakdown of old assumptions, then the higher perception of lawful ordering of the universe must be adopted.

Soviet Marxist-Leninist doctrine accommodates to the conflict between doctrine and reality of practice by means of the rationalization which Marx's own construction includes: the principle that the ordered development of society ought to be determined by the ordering of increasing intensity of capital-formation according to the principle of increasing basic scientific and derived technological progress. It is on that point that official Soviet Marxism-Leninism opens the door to policy-determinations consistent with reality.

The significance of this is made clearer, with respect to the Soviet case, by contrasting the sort of Leninist current of Soviet policy-making with the almost Maoist antagonism to industrial-scientific transformation associated with N. Bukharin.

Bukharin is the direct opposite to Lenin in respect of the crucial point being elaborated here. Lenin's underlying characteristic, shaping his use of Marxist influences, was Tchernyshevskian voluntarism—just as the leading Mensheviks noted, and complained loudly enough during the 1920s and 1930s. Bukharin used the formalities of actual and counterfeit Marxism to serve a different sort of underlying motivation. Bukharin was essentially a true "left" communist of the British-Jesuit variety.

A few leading facts concerning Bukharin pinpoint the shaping of his underlying outlook.

Bukharin came into the orbit of his immediate superior in the British-Hapsburg intelligence service, Parvus (Alexander Helphand), through his studies with the same Vienna circles that produced von Mises, and, later, Friedrich von Hayek, and Milton Friedman. That locates the circumstances of his assimilation into British intelligence, into

circles which would have placed him within the
Mont Pelerin Society branch of British-Jesuit intelligence today. From there, he became associated
with another product of the Vienna circle, Rudolf
Hilferding, representing, as a result of this indoctrination, a predecessor form of Cambridge University "systems philosophy" of today.

In Russia, he was associated with the anarchist
youth fringe of the Bolsheviks around Moscow
and came directly under Parvus's control during
the period preceding the 1917 Revolution, together
with the Vienna-based G. Ryazanov, and Karl
Radek.

L.D. Trotsky, an anarchosyndicalist of somewhat different track record, also intersected Parvus's control and the Vienna Warburg-Schiff et al.
control of elements of the Russian radicals. Trotsky's *Vienna Pravda* period is relevant, as is also
Lenin's prewar denunciation of Trotsky as an
immoral scalawag—Lenin's views were entirely
justified in fact on this point, as well as his
abhorrence of the Parvus-Trotsky doctrine of
"Permanent Revolution."

Lenin was essentially anti-oligarchist, whereas
Bukharin was a pro-oligarchist subagent of the
Parvus network. Lenin was for the industrial
development of Russia, preferably its capitalist
development and later, reluctantly, its socialist
industrial development. Bukharin's anticapitalist
Bolshevism was essentially pro-oligarchist anti-

industrialism, akin to the proruralist doctrine of the Maoists.

The survivors of the Parvus network became either Trotskyists (for example, G. Rakovsky, et al.) or, first, the "right opposition" (for example, Bukharin, Ryazanov, et al.), and then assimilated into the "right-wing Social-Democratic" apparatus of their mother organization, the Jewish-financier, subordinate element of the Anglo-American-Jesuit oligarchical intelligence establishment. In the United States, they orbit around, alternatively, the Coalition for a Democratic Majority and Georgetown University.

The same point is underscored by examining the origins of the mass-based components of fascist regimes, such as the Nazis and Mussolini's fascists.

The oligarchical anticapitalist, including his rentier-financier ally, attacks the capitalist-republican order and institutions of nations through a combination of Benthamite Jacobinism, such as today's environmentalists, and fascist movements which absorb the same sort of anarchist communist as Mussolini evolved out of the left wing of the Socialist Party of Italy, and as the Nazis drew upon the countercultural, "environmentalist" *Wandervogeln* of Weimar Germany.

The "left" variety of anarchist adopts the name of "Marxist anticapitalism"; the "right" variety of anarchist formation takes the guise of being an instrument for imposing fascist austerity on behalf of nominally capitalist financiers, such as Hjalmar Schacht or the "libertarians" such as Milton Friedman and Friedrich von Hayek. At bottom, they are both the same thing, with the same underlying impulses, which differ only as the same tool may be employed by its master in a different style.

Just so, since 1966-1968, the entire "left" in the United States has become overtly a fascist rabble, dedicated to the fascist Malthusian doctrine of environmentalism, and with homosexual-feminist and other cults that are direct echoes of the Nazi cults.

In dealing with social movements and with nations, it is indispensable to examine them on the two levels we have outlined here. One must deal concurrently with both levels, recognizing which is of relatively episodic significance for practice, and which more fundamental for the longer pull.

5

WHY
MILTON FRIEDMAN
IS A FRAUD

Since the assassination of President William
McKinley by a guest of Emma Goldman's New
York City Henry Street Settlement House, the
United States has never achieved significant rates
of economic progress except through the stimulus
of a war economy. Yet, since British intelligence's
Mont Pelerin Society launched its massive "free
enterprise" brainwashing campaign through the
Heritage Foundation, during May-June 1978,
thousands of otherwise sane and sensible conservatives have taken to lapsing periodically into
episodic brainwashed fits at the mention of the
trigger-word "free enterprise."

The ostensibly stimulating effect of war economy has not been overlooked entirely by the
principal, Georgetown-based advisers of former
Governor Ronald Reagan. They, and some others
who do not admire Georgetown particularly, have
joined a clamor which argues that after the United
States has been collapsed into a depression, the

launching of a war-economy drive will put the economy right. But, in almost the same breath, while proposing war-economy and other sorts of emergency regulation, these same fellows—or, at least, most of them—continue babbling the rhythmic pedal-point, "free enterprise built the United States." They mean by "free enterprise" what used to be called "free trade."

The present-day proponents of depression followed by war economy have in mind the appearances of the 1929-1945 period. After stumbling miserably through the persisting Depression of the 1930s, which no one seemed to be able to solve, the deployment of war production in 1940 mobilized creaking, worn-out productive capital and our labor force's depleted skills, such that by 1943 we had essentially achieved the combination of military mobilization and production-goals projected at the outset.

Yet, in admiring the 1940-1945 performance, we must not overlook the debt we piled up during the war, nor the postwar inflation triggered by that debt. It is not the production of military goods per se which caused the 1940-1945 recovery from the Depression. Military goods are, economically, waste, a purely inflationary expansion of the "overhead expenses" of the economy. (We shall say more on that in a moment.) There had to have been some other, correlative feature of war mobilization which accounts for the effective mobilization of productive powers.

Let us focus on World War II, noting that the World War I mobilization was the chief precedent of reference for the design of the World War II mobilization, and that the Korean War boom and the Vietnam War expenditures are related cases. Although military goods are the most conspicuous feature of a war-production boom, that feature tends more to mask, than to reveal the features of a war economy which promote economic mobilization. After we have reviewed those matters, we shall turn our attention to the unworkability of the sort of proposals recently and currently flowing from the precincts of the Committee on the Present Danger and Georgetown.

There were two principal features of the World War II war mobilization to be considered: First, the issuance of prime and secondary production contracts, matched by the organization of flows of cheap credit from the federal government through the private banking system to discount these war-production orders; second, the maintenance of a policy of "fair profits" and "fair wages."

Let us put aside, for the moment, the specifics of rationing and other mechanics of the Office of Price Administration (OPA), for example, as a mode of regulating "fair profits" and "fair wages." Let us consider the economic principles involved, not the obscene way this was managed under wartime conditions.

It is the war production credit system which was crucial to the success of the process. Given a

market, and an established consensus among pro-
ducers-investors on the desirability and assumed
durability of that market, the government's inter-
vention to supply flows of low-priced credit for
such productive investment through local banks of
the private-banking system will produce boom
conditions.

As to how more sensible assurance of fair profits
and wages would function, in contrast to OPA-
like measures, two references are most useful: the
success of American trucking under the regulatory
arrangements now being destroyed, and the success of the American agricultural system under
effective 100 percent parity conditions. Regulated
trucking, aided by the development of the Inter-
state Highway System, made U.S. trucking the
most efficient in the world, also reducing both the
average social cost for a ton-mile of average
freight, and reducing the amount of in-progress
unsold inventory accumulation required for each
level of gross national output of tangible product.

The development of markets, combined with
effects of near-parity prices enabled U.S. agriculture, combined with the benefits of the agricultural
extension system, cheap and abundant energy, and
industrial (agribusiness high-technology inputs) to
achieve the lowest social costs of food, by a wide
margin, over any other nation of the world.

The problem of war production as such is that
since military goods are neither household-con-

sumption goods (generally speaking), not useful productive capital, they do not lead to regeneration of the productive powers of the economy through their consumption. They do not function to aid the increased output of production or productivity. *Therefore, they are not true wealth.* Hence, the credit issued against military production must be secured by taxing real wealth production outside the military sphere. Hence, war-production stimulants are intrinsically inflationary.

If the war-production system approach were applied to production of export capital-goods, which are wealth, no such inflationary side-effect occurs. If the production of export capital-goods is profitable, the amount of wealth produced exceeds significantly the combined principal and interest costs of the credit employed for financing such export production.

One should compare those observations immediately and directly with the contents of three key reports to the first Congress of the United States, on credit, banking, and manufactures, by Treasury Secretary Alexander Hamilton. This comparison immediately leads us to the answer we require.

The apparent success of war-production periods for the U.S. economy during this century to date is not—and could not be—the consequence of the inherently inflationary production of military goods themselves. The point to be made is that

*only under war mobilization conditions has the
United States during this century adopted even a
deformed version of what used to be termed the
"American System" of political economy.*

Under all other circumstances, the United States
has been in an actual, or imminent state of inflationary (secular) decline or depression. The 1922-
1926 and 1954-1957 periods are exemplary of
short-lived periods of apparent, relative, non-war-
economy prosperity which proved to be merely an
accumulation of the preconditions for a subsequent depression or major recession. Under these
other circumstances, the United States's policy has
been effectively modeled on the British System of
political economy.

Broadly, the history of the conflict between the
American and British systems of political economy
within the United States has been as follows.

Over the period from the election of the first
George Washington administration, until the election of Thomas Jefferson, Hamiltonian institutions
of credit, banking, and promotion of manufactures
not only pulled the United States out of bank-
ruptcy, but transformed the nation into an emi-
nently credit-worthy and expanding economy,
whose achievements were the admiration of much
of continental Europe and greatly feared by the
British.

Although Jefferson, under the influence of British agent Albert Gallatin, immediately proceeded

to tear apart the institutions of credit, banking, and investment-fostering, as well as defense capabilities, the first period under Jefferson continued to show the left-over benefits of the preceding decade. Under the second Jefferson administration and that of Madison, the U.S. economy declined precipitously, slipping over to the British model as outlined by Adam Smith's *Wealth of Nations*.

The second period of successful economic development of the United States began in 1818, and tended to the conclusion of the presidency of John Quincy Adams. This recovery followed a period of near-collapse of the U.S. economy, a collapse economist Mathew Carey proved to have been caused directly by the adoption of Smith's polices (see Allen Salisbury, *The Civil War and the American System*, 1978, pp. 385-427). The recovery centered around combined support for a return to Hamiltonian policies under Nicholas Biddle's direction of the Second Bank of the United States, and the qualitative improvement of West Point by incorporation of the advances effected in France by Lazare Carnot. A rapid recovery of U.S. credit and economy ensued.

The election of Andrew Jackson caused an accelerating decline in the real aspects of the U.S. economy. Central to this was Jackson's undermining of the Bank of the United States, to place control of banking and national credit in the hands of London-allied, Manhattan bankers headed by

Jackson's patron Martin van Buren. This led to the Panic of 1837, a direct result of the return to Smith's "free trade" doctrine.

The relative position of the U.S. economy declined, despite Westward-expansion growth, over the period from 1830 to 1860. The combination of New England and Manhattan merchant and banking interests, plus the slave-owners' faction, pursued a "free trade" policy that looted both U.S. industry and free agriculture, looting the United States in favor of Britain. The core of resistance to this on-going ruin of the United States was located among Midwestern grain farmers, substantially of German origin, who formed the base of Abraham Lincoln's Whig faction within the combination of forces that composed the Republican Party of the 1860s.

Lincoln used the conditions of war to effect a massive industrialization of the United States, a policy he intended to extend as reconstruction of the southern states had he not been assassinated by the British Secret Intelligence Service's Booth, with complicity of the Jesuits of Georgetown and the Manhattan financier interests centered then around Rothschild representative August Belmont and Seligman.

Andrew Johnson veered toward the policies of Jefferson and Jackson, institutionalizing a relative backwardness of southern states which persisted until the aftermath of World War II. Grant was captured by the Manhattan banking interests. The ruin of Jay Cooke ended the Lincoln efforts to restore national banking. The 1879 Specie Resumption Act placed control of U.S. credit under the control of a group of Manhattan bankers allied to London. The subsequent establishment of the Federal Reserve System, modeled on designs based on the Bank of England, consolidated this foreign control of U.S. credit—and debt—by supranational, London-centered interests.

However, despite the monstrous, increasing subversion of national credit and banking by London agents, the industrial revolution set into motion by Lincoln was eroded, not fully stopped, until the Versailles Treaty and its aftermath. The closing-down of Ellis Island's free-entry policies signaled the fact that the industrial-expansionist phase of the post-1860 economy had ended.

Since then, we have had the following periods of relative prosperity: 1922-1926, 1940-1945, 1949-1953, 1954-1957, 1962-1966. The years 1922 to 1926 and 1954 to 1957 were the only periods of apparent non-war-economy expansion during the post-Versailles period. The periods 1940 to 1945 and 1949 to 1953 were war-economy phases pure and simple. The interim 1962 to 1966 was a blend of semirecovery, based on the combined effects of the National Aeronautics and Space Administration, the Vietnam War, and related expenditures.

Some so-called economists would disagree. The

ostensible empirical basis for their objections is GNP data.

Let us now summarize, afresh here, the ABCs of political economy which show the fraudulent quality of GNP-related methods of national income and product accounting. Having done that, we shall match the economic side, comparable to Hamilton's 1791 *Report to Congress on the Subject of Manufactures,* with the credit and banking complements. With that apparatus developed here, we shall conclude with a twofold criticism of Friedmanism. We shall show why Friedman is a fraud, and also account for the mechanisms of credulity which prompt numbers of conservatives, among others, to regard themselves as Friedmanites.

ABCs of National Economic Accounting

The failure of Adam Smith's *Wealth of Nations* as a guide to understanding both the success of the U.S. political economy under Washington, and related breakthroughs introduced to France by Lazare Carnot, prompted British intelligence to foster a fresh approach by David Ricardo. Although the latter portion of Ricardo's famous *Principles* exhibits more of his "nervous breakdown" of that period than economic sense, the book as a whole performs the function of abstracting from the combined American, French, and

British experience of the preceding period, to produce an approximately sound set of accounting categories for study of national economies.

Later, during the nineteenth century, John Stuart Mill's "utilitarianism" and the influence of Marshallian doctrine pushed aside Ricardo. Consequently, the active use of Ricardo's accounting categories today has been, mistakenly, attributed to Karl Marx's borrowing from Ricardo's work.

The validity of Ricardo's work on this point is limited almost entirely to the almost common-sensical appropriateness of the accounting categories themselves. Although Marx's plagiarism of Friedrich List, to correct Ricardo from the standpoint of "labor-power," did effect improvements for analysis over Ricardo's use of the accounting categories, both Ricardo's and Marx's efforts to equate the data with a notion of "value" are flawed, a failure.

Hence, the reader must not object to the fact that we employ those common-sensically sound accounting categories in a way contrary to either Ricardo's or Marx's notion of the values to be associated with such data. Although the corrections we employ are the writer's own, as effected beginning 1952, the writer's method is the same as that of Leibniz, Monge, Carnot. Hence it is mistaken to view the writer as having superseded Marx. Marx represents a retreat in economic science from the preceding, scientific competence typified by Leibniz, Hamilton, the Careys, Ferrier, Chaptal, Dupin, and Friedrich List. The writer's advances are to be located in respect to the latter group of scientific thinkers.

The essential, correct notion of *wealth* is derived from demographical analysis of a reconstructed history of the rise of civilization from savagery and barbarism. That is, *wealth* is not something unto itself. It assumes the quality of wealth as it efficiently mediates, through its consumption, an increase in the population-potentials of a society. *In brief, wealth is measured as it mediates an increase in the possible population-density of a society at higher per capita standards of consumption and culture.*

A short space ahead, we shall prove this notion in a more rigorous, altogether conclusive way. For the moment, the brief definition given is sufficient.

The activities of a society relative to effecting rises in population-potential are of two forms, properly distinguished as *productive* and *necessary nonproductive* activities of the population. The first corresponds to the *production* of *tangible* wealth; the second is the "overhead expense" typified by administration and services, assumed required by production.

Administration pertains to the net result conceivable as the *organization* of the productive and distributive processes. Services include, in addition to protective activities such as military, fire, police, positive services such as sanitation, medicine, teaching, and the production-related activities associated with science and engineering. The services pertain to the cultivation of the technological qualities of human productive activity. Since the benefits of these services are counted once in terms of per capita output of tangible wealth from production, to count services as wealth would be a crude blunder of double-counting.

We now review, once again, the ABCs of the accounting procedures for assessing the performance of a national economy.

First, the only competent approach to accounting for the total income and product of an economy is to treat the entirety of the economy as if it were a single business enterprise.

Second, we begin with demographic analysis of the economy, to arrive at the correspondence between households and members of households modally part of the labor force as that society defines its labor force.

For example, the United States today demands a labor force qualified by a period of maturation of youth reaching to between the eighteenth and twenty-second year, as corresponding to development of an adequately skilled entrant into the labor force by accepted standards of culture and educational practice. (We are obliged to employ pre-1960 standards for this, since educational "reforms" and other changes in circumstances of youth effected over the past two decades represent a devolution of educational and other relevant institutions.) We have, for the moment, institutionalized an alterable but still-enforced notion of retirement age. Then still define the family-structure of households, respecting the roles of wife and mother, to define the modal determination of potential wage-earner.

We, then, define households by the corresponding form of employment of the potential wage-earners (members of the modal labor force).

This seems to involve some acounting difficulties, since wage-earners from the same household may be in variously productive and nonproductive categories, and may change their employment from one to the other. True, no exact determination can be made, for just such reasons. However, as the reader shall soon discover, it is the shifts in the ratios of productive and nonproductive forms of employment which are the primary data of competent economic analysis, not absolute, scalar values. So, it is merely essential that we be consistent in the way we account for the correspondence between productive and nonproductive households; there is no point in attempting to split hairs for the purpose of coming to an absolute distinction among the categorization of households themselves.

We then define the demographic (household)

categories in terms of the analysis of the tangible-wealth output of production. It is at this point that we introduce the accounting categories as such.

We apportion the total output of tangible wealth, produced by productive labor, among the following three principal accounting categories: (1) Symbol C—the costs of regenerating (replenishing) the productive capital consumed by combined obsolescence and consumption for total current output of tangible wealth. This includes improvements in land, plant, equipment, machinery, semifinished product inventory, materials, supplies, and energy; (2) Symbol V—the cost of maintaining the material and cultural level of the households corresponding to the total productive sector of the labor force, whether actually employed or not. This means, in fact, a material cost allowing for technological competence of the labor force to assimilate advances in productive techniques which are imminent; (3) Symbol S—Gross Profit, the remainder to output of tangible wealth after deducting allocations for C and V.

The combined cost of waste plus administration and services, including their capital costs, is designated by a subcategory of S, symbol d—*nonproductive consumption*, or the "overhead expense" of the society (economy). Subtracting d from S defines the "net profit" of the society (economy), which we symbolize by S'.

We have three basic ratio-parameters derived from this:

(1) $S/(C+V)$: national productivity;
(2) $S'/(C+V)$: rate of profit of national economy;
(3) C/V: capital-intensity of production.

Expansion of the economy is expressed in this accounting as the "reinvestment" of S' for either or a combination of: (a) expansion of the economy in scale; (b) increasing the capital-intensity of production, C/V. *Failure to so "reinvest" all of S' is a dysfunction of circulation.*

Analysis of the economy begins by studying the changes in the values of the ratios $S/(C+V)$, $S'/(C+V)$, and C/V. *We place special emphasis on correlating changes in* C/V *with changes in* $S/(C+V)$ *and* $S'/(C+V)$.

GNP Is Bunk as a Measure of Growth

The foregoing already indicates, conclusively enough, why it is peddling sheer buncombe to argue that an economy is growing because the current (or constant) dollar value of its total GNP has increased. It is only the output of tangible wealth which measures absolute scalar growth.

Whether growth is sustainable depends upon the ratio $S'/(C+V)$. The rate of profit and rate of potential growth are equivalent terms *in first ap-*

proximation. A "zero-profit" economy is a "zero-growth" economy, *and vice versa.*

If productivity [$S/(C+V)$] is being maintained, or rising, then the rate of growth of $d/(C+V)$ determines the value of $S'/(C+V)$. In other words, an increase in combined administration and services employment, if productive employment is constant, comes out as an increase in d, and therefore a reduction in the rate of profit $S'/(C+V)$. If there is a shift from productive to administrative plus services employment, the society is headed toward collapse under conditions of constant or slightly rising values for $S/(C+V)$.

Since 1957, there has been a secular shift of employment. In brief, the U.S. economy has been forms, with at best about 7 percent trends in rise in productivity during the early 1960s, and a lowering of the rate of growth of productivity after 1965-1966. Since 1971-1974, there has been a shift from energy-dense to labor-intensive productive employment, combined with an accelerated overall shift from productive to nonproductive employment. In brief, the U.S. economy has been collapsing at an accelerating rate.

All of this is usually pedantically reported from Washington as accompanied by a continued growth in the GNP.

Hence all the university programs of instruction in economics are currently profoundly incompetent, and nearly all popularly accredited working economists and related "think tanks" are also incompetent.

The General Imbecility of Milton Friedman

The Carter administration, like the early and post-August 1971 phases of the Nixon administration, is committed to Friedmanite policies. Friedmanism is the popularized version of a doctrine which is not economics at all, but is properly termed "monetarism." Derived from this buncombe is the doctrine of "fiscal austerity," the nonsense-doctrine that it is the growth of monetary aggregates, a matter related to the size of the federal budget deficits, which governs rates of inflation.

On the contrary, as the foregoing summary of competent national-income accounting indicates, it is the direction of flows of monetary aggregates, not the size of such aggregates, which determines whether or not the ratios $S/(C+V)$ and $S'/(C+V)$ are growing or contracting.

To be concrete. At present, the effective borrowing costs of capital far exceed the rate of return on particular capital investments. This means that credit flows away from capital-formation toward high-gain rentier speculation, while shrinking the productive base of the U.S. dollar. Therefore, "fiscal austerity" does not combat inflation, but does directly the opposite. It causes a tendency for increased rates of inflation accompanied and fueled by contraction of the productive base. In other words, it produces an accelerating hyperinflationary collapse, which continues until combined collapse of the economy and monetary system altogether destroys the national currency.

What is wanted to correct this are changes in the direction of flow of monetary aggregates. The monetary aggregates must, in fact, be substantially increased to scales consistent with high rates of deflating forms of capital-intensive productive investment. Credit, at relatively low prime borrowing costs, must be copiously supplied for sound farms and industries, while nonproductive flows must be constricted. In other words, the power of the federal government to tax income selectively, and to order selective flows of credit, giving adequate preferences to productive investment and relative penalties for nonproductive, is the only remedy for the present situation.

The liar and incompetent Friedman protests that such "dirigist" measures interfere with the "freedom of the marketplace." He holds up the case of Hong Kong and Chile as examples of the success of his policies.

Hong Kong's economy is based on two leading elements. First, it processes annually more than $10 billion of revenues from the international illegal opium traffic. Second, it processes virtually slave-labor from Communist China. Both arrangements are among the most regulated markets of the world—so much for the Hong Kong "free marketplace."

Chile is a nasty fascist dictatorship, a hideous copy of Nazi Germany. The core of the Pinochet regime's apparatus is provided by dyed-in-the-wool Nazis, who have never abandoned that political profession since their direct affiliations to Nazi Germany of the 1930s.

Granted, externally, the Chilean currency has seemed to improve since the coup of 1973. If Friedman proposes to argue that Friedmanite economics produced a miracle there, he is lying.

The pre-1973 collapse of Chile's economy under Allende was rigged from the outside by economic warfare measures, including artificial depression of copper prices for Chile's exports and international banking conditions dictated to the nation. Once Allende had been overthrown with aid of such destabilizing economic and monetary warfare, the economic warfare against the Chilean government was terminated.

Furthermore, two additional Friedmanite observations concerning Pinochet's Chile are also lies.

He argues that Pinochet has solved most of the internal problem of inflation (as distinct from externally caused inflation). This is a lie. Pinochet has used Friedman's imitation of the doctrine and practice of Nazi Economics Minister Hjalmar Schacht to turn continuing high rates of inflation against the economic base of the economy. That is, instead of eliminating the cause of a, for example, 20 percent rate of inflation, compensate for that rate of inflation by gouging 20 percent that year out of the productive capital and incomes of the economy.

He also lies, insisting that no savage assault on incomes has occurred. The fact is that about one-third of the Chilean population is now categorized by the Pinochet government's economic advisers as "useless eaters," which the advisers now propose to eliminate in some way yet to be precisely determined.

What Friedmanism amounts to in actuality is the insistence that institutions of self-government be prevented from interfering with a dictatorship over credit, markets, and investment exerted by a private cartel of rentier-financiers. This is what "free trade" meant in the pen of East India Company scribbler Adam Smith. It is precisely what it means in the instance of Friedman or von Hayek.

One has but to compare Hamilton's reports to the Congress on credit, banking, and manufactures, and to recognize that these policies flowed directly from the requirements of constitutional government.

It is the purpose of self-government to enable a people to freely shape their own destinies, free of the encroachments of any overreaching foreign or domestic power which might seek to place itself at a higher level of authority in any matter than self-government. This means, above all, the power and responsibility of self-government to provide the preconditions for expression of individual freedom. These include a gold-backed, stable national currency issued by the federal government, a supply of credit for worth purposes as low borrowing costs, and protection of production and trade to ensure fair profits and fair wages for those productive ventures which contribute to overall national profitability, growth, and strength of the nation and its economy.

The power of central banking is a monstrously great and efficient power over the very means of life of the individual. Such central banking is unavoidable for a modern economy. The question is solely whether we choose to make such power accountable through means of self-government, or abandon ourselves to the dictatorship of a private consortium of rentier-financiers?

More on Economics

In a reconstruction of modes of production typical of various phases of the emergence of civilization we show that the amount of energy throughput per capita increases in correspondence to the successive advances. Moreover, the rate of increase of the energy-throughput per capita also rises over this span.

This fact, placing economic analysis within the domain of thermodynamics, demarcates the point of division between mere accounting and what is actually economics. We summarize the leading point here, to illustrate the fact that Friedman, von Hayek, and other sorts of university programs in economics today absolutely ignore those issues and conceptions which are determining for economics. Conversely, we show that Alexander Hamilton was a true economist, whereas the fraud, Adam Smith, was not in fact.

The significance of the historical increase of energy-throughputs is introduced by repeating here the following refutation of the myth of "natural resources"!

What is usually meant by "natural resources," especially by the physiocrats of the past and the neo-Malthusians of today, is the false, stated or implied assertion that a set of classes of well-defined objects in "nature" constitutes a finite mass of "resources." The correlated, physiocratic, assumption is that this array of object-classes constitutes the ultimate, finite source of the world's wealth. That point is sometimes extended further, as in Henry A. Kissinger's proposal of the "International Energy Agency" and "Common Fund," that the profit of the world is reducible to the "rent" extracted from lending the exploitation of such "natural resources."

In fact, "natural resources" are defined for any body of productive practice as those aspects of nature which can be used for the production of

wealth at acceptable social costs for their exploitation. For example, a cubic mile of the earth's
surface contains a substantial portion of the total
mineral resources the world requires presently for
a year's production. Combining such resources
with recycling of waste, the notion of limits of
resources begins to be dissipated, but a different
conception occurs in its place.

Since the business of processing mineral ores is
essentially the application of heat at varying levels
of temperature-equivalent (energy-flux density), it
is readily seen that what constitutes an economical
ore is a matter of the level of technology, with
emphasis on the social cost of rising levels of
energy-flux density.

So, in general, the notion of "natural resources"
is merely a relative conception, relative to progress
in technology. Furthermore, as the illustration
states, technological progress can be ranked in
terms of social costs of rising energy-flux densities
for increasing per capita energy-throughput.

However, if a society were to accept "zero
technological growth," then the relative limits of
resources would take the form of de facto depletion
of a finite mass of such resources.

Hence, as Hamilton elaborated the same essential argument in popularized forms of eighteenth-
century facts, the sole source of wealth is the
realization of continuing advances in science and
technology in the form of those rising productive

powers of labor associated with increasing use of "artificial labor." "Artificial labor" is productive capital embodying advances in technology, and conduiting rising per capita energy-throughputs, at rising values of energy-flux density, into a form useful in the productive process. In other words, rising rates of capital-intensity under conditions of increasing per capita energy-throughput and energy-flux densities.

With adequate increases in both energy-throughput per capita and in energy-flux densities, there are no limits to resources economically available to man. The only limitations are advances in basic scientific knowledge and the rates of realization of those benefits as investment of new productive technologies.

My own important breakthrough in scientific economics has been to locate the means for comprehending deterministic analysis of economic processes through use of the Riemannian hydrothermodynamics of a multiply-connected manifold to reduce energy, technology, and accounting-ratios for an economy to a form of quantitative analysis admitting of solutions.

The real "savings" of an economy are not its money-savings, but the magnitude S'. The function of a credit-banking system is to supply a combination of money-savings and fiat credit to enable the circulation for productive reinvestment of the margin of output S'.

To accomplish this at stable, low borrowing costs, the state must establish a stable currency. No way has been discovered to do this but by providing gold backing for that currency. That is, as long as the imbalances incurred on net account, after balancing sales against purchases, of the transactions in a national currency are covered by the offering of gold at the competitive price of production of gold for monetary purposes, the currency in use is as good as gold.

There is no error in the state's creation of fiat credit—as through the issue of banknotes against a deficit in the federal budget. This is sound as long as the deficit-issue is used as credit extended for the production of wealth, and as long as the wealth created carries a value which exceeds the combined debt and a competitive rate of profit. In that case, the debt has merely mediated the realization of S' within the national economy as new wealth exceeding S' in value.

The way in which this is done under the American System is in cooperation with local private banks. In the total realization of S' as new productive investment, a mixture of advanced risk-equity, loaned savings, and credit created by the federal government is combined for the financing of the investment. This mixture ensures that the combined federal and private banking have caused the borrower to pledge his equity-advance as a margin of risk on account of his own productive performance. The federal bankers have the assurance of the private banker's risk of savings lent that the banker is lending in a prudent manner.

This is accomplished by providing levels of income to particular persons and firms above the values of C, V and $(C+V)$ definable, at least implicitly, as the barebones values for those items. These increments provide a source of allocable savings over current purchases, to become either equity or private-bank savings.

This creation of credit is properly accomplished by the banking institutions of the governments of republics. However, private banking systems also have the power to do this, if government does not prevent that usurpation of the proper functions of government.

If a private banking system, such as the British-centered system represented by the Federal Reserve System, secures control of the debt of nations, all sorts of monstrosities can, and usually do ensue. Instead of creating credit as banknotes, balanced by credit for productive investment of borrowers from the federal bank, the government borrows funds at interest from the private banking system, relying on fluctuations of interest rates established in private financial markets. The power to create credit and currency is then shifted into hands of the private financiers' cartel, and the government borrower is transformed from a sovereign entity into a tax-farm to be looted through rigging of private markets by rentier finance.

When monetary processes are comprehended

from the vantage-point we have outlined here, all the mystification vanishes. It becomes clear that not only Milton Friedman is a babbling, fascist fraud. (He does admit, correctly, that his doctrines are an emulation of those of Nazi Economics Minister Hjalmar Schacht.)

How the Conservative Is Conned by Friedman

Taking Friedman's televised lectures as a point of reference, we can sum up the way in which the credulous admirers of Friedman have duped themselves.

First, Friedman invents "facts" as the plausibility of his assertion seems to require this. The Hong Kong and Chile cases are exemplary.

Second, Friedman argues his case by means of hypothetical cases, which cases depend upon the assumption that the microcosm of buying and selling by small groups of firms and individuals can be extrapolated, without the slightest actual consideration of economics, to a purely monetary doctrine covering entire economies.

Why Georgetown's "War-Economy" Scheme Must Fail

By using a combination of GNP methods of accounting and purely fraudulent assertions concerning the state of Soviet technology and economy generally, a group intersecting the Georgetown University Center for Strategic and International Studies (CSIS) has proposed to (1) put the U.S. economy into a depression-collapse during 1980; and then (2) construct a U.S. war-economy "recovery" modeled on the mid-1930s arguments of Nazi boss Hermann Goering. Associated with this is a maniacal gleam in the eyes of the proponents, the thought that Nazi Germany came close to conquering the Soviet Union during World War II.

At the best, the whole conception is chiefly a wishful delusion.

A few cases in point indicate the problems.

There is, presently, a crisis in secret communications, caused by the fact that Soviet computer software has qualitatively surpassed U.S. software technology in key areas of application. As a result, small Soviet computers can accomplish decoding of secret NATO signals just as efficiently as the NATO forces can accomplish such a task with qualitatively larger computers.

The Soviets have developed a "rapid-fire laser," which deployed, will be waiting to use subsonic Cruise missiles for target-practice by the time those missiles are significantly deployed.

The Soviets are reported by the most authoritative intelligence sources to be about one year short of deploying "particle beam weapons" suited to destroying ICBMs in the ascent phase—before real or counterfeit warheads are deployed.

Those are exemplary of the trend in Soviet "state of the art" advances over NATO.

The most significant background fact to be considered in this connection is the comparable numbers of scientists and engineers produced, as well as employed in basic research and development, especially since the post-1966 sharp downturn in the United States.

The Soviet economy does have significant problems. The worst single problem relative to the U.S.A., is the lag in Soviet agriculture—a U.S. advantage which Carter, Volcker, and others are on the verge of destroying. Otherwise, the combination of economic warfare and potential added measures of such warfare against the Soviet economy by the NATO alliance obliges Soviet planners to avoid critical dependency on a rational international division of labor. This creates a capital shortage, relatively speaking, in the economy, since the density of required capital investment in the Soviet economy is driven higher than for nations participating in a broader-based division of international labor.

Soviet planning was adversely affected by the influences of Cambridge University's "systems philosophy," from about the mid-sixties onward. The associated bias toward low-risk-fact "cost-benefit" policies must curtail the benefits of "frontier" allocations, which, although deemed high-risk investments, are the sole source of high rates of growth productivity. This influence appears to have been curtailed over the recent year's-end, in favor of the influence of high-technology military-scientific currents.

Finally, as noted, use of GNP standards prompts Western analysts to grossly underestimate the relative growth-rates and performances of the Soviet vis-à-vis NATO economies.

The remarkable element in such comparisons is not modest Soviet economic progress-rates over the past two decades. Compared with a healthy U.S. and Western European economy, the Soviet growth-rates would be relatively unimpressive, and most unimpressive compared with the best recent period of Japan's economy.

The remarkable element in the comparison is the way in which the United States and Britain have been destroying their industrial economies over the course of the past two decades, especially since the mid-1960s, and dragging down the economies of their allies significantly as a result.

At present levels, the U.S. economy as a whole is presently operating at a loss, and being driven lower, below breakeven by Carter's energy conservation policies, even before the rash of recent, fascist-modeled austerity measures. If we destroy Chrysler and a number of other major and small industrial firms, destroy our agriculture as is presently being done, the possibility of U.S. economic recovery is wrecked for the medium-term. Over the course of the 1980s, the United States would become a second-rate power relative to the Soviet Union, and would have dragged Germany and Japan into economic chaos by shrinking their Middle East and other developing-sector basic export-markets with International Monetary Fund "conditionalities" and World Bank "appropriate technologies" policies.

1980 is not 1940. The United States is essentially in worse basic condition as an economy today, relative to current state-of-the-art technology, than it was at the end of the last Depression. We lack the industrial base to sustain a war-economy boom on even scales relatively lower than those of 1940-1943.

In addition to the state of the economy as such, we lack the quality of population we had available in 1940. We are demographically aged, having become so over the past two decades of decline in population growth. The literacy of our population's youth is significantly lower than that of 1940, with the spreading use of marijuana and other drugs, as well as the drug culture destroying a large plurality of the future labor force. This coincides with both an orientation away from technology, and a qualitative decline in the intangible, but decisive moral qualities of the youth population.

As for our military "think-tankers," not one of them is to be credited even with minimal honesty concerning extent or projectable U.S. military capability. If there were honest and sane, they would have torn the Congress apart over the issue of the raging drug-usage in our military services. We would have had a series of tough court-martial sentences passed out for the use of a single joint of marijuana. That such a demand has not been forthcoming is adequate evidence of the lack of either courage or simple morality among influential military ranks.

Unless there is an immediate adoption of the policies associated uniquely with my presidential campaign, the point at which Moscow deploys particle-beam weapons is the point at which the United States becomes a second-rate military power, as well as a relic of its former economic power. The circles controlling our strategic, scientific, and economic policies are suicidal lunatics —which would be commendable if they were not taking the rest of us with them.

6

'FREEDOM' VERSUS 'ANARCHISM'

If much of their variously written and oral arguments were to be isolated from other, contradictory evidence of their beliefs and behavior, a conclusive case could be made that numerous among self-styled conservatives have no comprehension of "freedom" either as an idea or for practice. An honest court, limiting itself to such selected evidence, would be obliged to convict and sentence such self-styled conservatives as raving anarchists.

That conviction and sentence would be justice for the cases of Al Stang's and Congressman Larry MacDonald's co-thinkers within the ranks of the John Birch Society, for most of the Ku Klux Klan membership, and similar cases. These, and like-minded folk, owe their dues to such entities as the anarchist sect, the Libertarian Party, in company with William F. Buckley and kindred sorts of pot-smoking fops. Except for the benefits of soap, and political equivalent of distinctions in regional dialects, the Libertarian Party, in turn, is barely distinguishable in political philosophy from the Citizens' Party of Barry Commoner, Chicago's Don Rose, and Jane Fonda. These folk truly have no notion of "freedom." They are raving anarchists, now well along the pathway to joining the anarchists who earlier followed Benito Mussolini and Adolf Hitler into fascism.

In other cases, I would enter *amicus curiae* support for appeal of an unjust sentence. I would argue that the conservatives in these other instances were not truly anarchists. I would submit evidence of their moral natures to prove this. I would admit that their written and oral statements, used to convict them earlier, had indeed been made. I would demonstrate that miseducation had been the cause of their repeating foolish statements, statements whose putative import was in direct conflict with their moral characteristics.

The Anti-Semitic Analogy

Otherwise, there is a parallel between such uses of anarchist phraseology by conservatives, and some conservatives' conditioning into verbal postures which border on the appearance of anti-Semitism.

It is a fact that the leading circles of the "Fact Finding" commission of B'nai B'rith's Anti-Defamation League are an evil collation, whose activity over the past decades has been chiefly to manufacture anti-Semites where none would have existed but for the ADL's libels and harassments against enraged honest citizens. It is also true that numerous Jewish dupes, otherwise innocent supporters of the ADL, have blindly refused to acknowledge overwhelming evidence of the ADL leadership's character. This credulous complicity has often made such Jewish dupes accomplices of the ADL leadership's crimes.

This behavior by the mere dupes of the ADL is like the same dupes' current support for the "settlements policy" of the Nazi-like, and indeed fascist, regime of Israel's Menachim Begin. Begin's government is doing to the Arab Palestinians what the Nazi "settlements policy" (*Siedlungspolitik*) perpetrated in Eastern Europe during the last war. Otherwise, the austerity which Israel imposes upon its own citizens, ostensibly in response to rising rates of triple-digit inflation, is identical with, and modeled wittingly upon the policies of Nazi Economics Minister Hjalmar Schacht.

The evidence of the fascist character of both the ADL leadership and of the Begin government is overwhelming, conclusive. Yet, out of impulses of "Jewish nationalism" fed to the point of hysteria by the combination of the Nazi experience and postwar Israeli developments, there are numerous Jewish-Americans, otherwise profoundly antifascist in their own deeper natures, who refuse more or less obsessively, to face overwhelming factual evidence in these two matters.

Some conservatives, including numerous who

despised anti-Semitism .vehemently at the close of the last war, have reacted to ADL-led persecution by becoming actually or proximately anti-Semitic. The ADL, having so created actual and ostensible anti-Semitism, where none previously existed, gloats over the results, raking in larger contributions from among duped Jewish-Americans who refuse to face facts.

These ADL-centered activities coincide in both appearance and fact with the Jewish names of certain rentier-financier interests—those banking houses that emerged, as a group, and continue to be mere *Hofjuden* for the historically anti-Semitic (in fact) black nobility of Europe. The case of Cliveden-Cecil-allied Ambassador Joseph P. Kennedy echoes the sort of anti-Semitism of such *Hofjuden*-allied oligarchs. Kennedy, wittingly dependent upon the patronage of Jewish-name rentier-banking interests of London and Manhattan, merely acquired the sentiments of the British and continental black nobility, in the manner typical of the parvenu's response to the patronage of the latter circles.

By allying with the British and black nobility oligarchs who merely use Jewish *Hofjuden* as expendable, talented instruments, the disoriented "Cold War" conservative compels himself, so to speak, to adduce a "Jewish conspiracy" from his own wishful distortion of the evidence. The ironies of the black nobility oligarchists center at Georgetown University underscore this aspect of the growth of anti-Semitism in the United States.

The case of Henry A. Kissinger illustrates the point.

Kissinger entered adolescence in a town outside Nuremberg, Germany: Fürth. The "Rothschild" of that region was one branch of the international oligarchist *Hofjuden* family of Oppenheimer-Oppenheim. It was this branch of the family which sponsored, during the First World War, the first application of *Siedlungspolitik* to Eastern Europe, through a member of the family serving in a high position with the Kaiser's government. This family was closely associated with the early phases of the Hitler regime; one member was celebrated by the Nazis for his aid in financing Nazi armaments build-up.

Since the first appearance of Kissinger's scandalous, conceptually illiterate doctoral dissertation at Harvard, under Professor William Yandell Elliott, and Kissinger's continued, obsessive emulation of Metternich and Bismarck since, it is clear that Henry has shaped his character around his perception of the Oppenheimer model during his adolescence.

Henry has come to visualize himself as a Jewish *Hofrat* of the continental European oligarchical court.

This masturbational element dominating Kissinger's career in public life was clearly activated into outer practice when the German oligarchist-turned-U.S. counterintelligence specialist (under General Julius Klein) Fritz Kraemer, elevated Henry from the status of Pfc. jeep-driver in occupied Germany, to a rising position within the lower ranks of U.S. intelligence. Saturation with oligarchist ideology at Harvard under Professor Elliott's patronage, and later indoctrination at Sussex (Tavistock) by the Psychological Warfare Executive of British intelligence, brought Henry's masturbational self-image as an upstart *Hofrat* forward. His adopted self-image as "acting President of the United States" since Nixon's credulous downgrading of Secretary William Rogers, has crystalized the dominant, masturbational element in Henry's personality to an acted-out obsession.

Henry is better understood by noting the essential equivalence of his character to that of the despised Jewish *Sonderkommando* in the Nazi concentration camps. This is otherwise the product of the "transference" phenomenon described by the psychoanalyst Bettelheim. In response to aggravated anti-Semitic persecution, a Jew of weak moral character chooses survival by becoming one of his persecutors. He becomes a "Manichean"—like Goethe's version of *Faust*—who sells his soul to Satan in expectation of such earthly paradise as he hopes Satan will offer him in return for aiding Satan's effort to secure his turn at ruling the world.

So, some conservatives have been influenced by

"Cold War" logic into ignoring the ordinary Jew, to construct an illusory image of a "Jewish conspiracy." They cling to this because their personal experience of the conspiratorial evils of the ADL leadership proves to them that some Jews are guilty of just the sort of evil the "Jewish conspiracy" myth transforms into a racial generalization.

The Myth of Anarchism

The same, flawed mechanisms of judgment governing the adoption of the "Jewish conspiracy" myth operate to prompt the substitution of the anarchist's notion of "freedom" for the republican principles of freedom.

The argument develops more or less as follows:

Point One: The agreed view is that the Soviet Union is a totalitarian state; government control of about everything.

Point Two: It is agreed that the fundamental conflict in the world is a struggle between "atheistic Communism" and "freedom."

Point Three: The professed special character of the Soviet Union is the "dictatorship of the proletariat," which is professedly centered around governmental control of the economy. This governmental control, centered in control over the economy, is "therefore" identified as the essence of the matter against which the cause of "freedom" must be fought.

In other words, just as in the case of the alleged

"Jewish conspiracy," a nest of successive *negations* is employed to arrive "rigorously" at what is falsely represented as a *positive* doctrine of "freedom."

The Devils Are Stirred Up

Historically, this sort of thinking has led to fascist totalitarianism—as exemplified by the cases of Mussolini's Italy and Nazi Germany. Yet, to propose that such views must always lead, in a linear fashion, toward fascism is the sort of *post hoc, ergo propter hoc* lunacy which Cambridge's Mrs. Joan Robinson, in one of her few good moments, rightly attributes to the imbecilic monetarist, Professor Milton Friedman.

Arguments of the sort we have summarily criticized here are not *the cause of* fascism. Such arguments have the significance of destroying those faculties of judgment which otherwise stand in the way of fascist impulses.

The subordination of the critical faculties of judgment for social and political practice to such forms of negativist "rigor" has the effect of degrading the conception of man and of the lawful ordering of the processes of nature to views which Dante Alighieri analyzes in the "Inferno" canticle of his *Commedia*. The characteristic form of misconception of man and nature which Dante outlines in that canticle is variously manifest as existentialism (Bernard of Clairvaux, Stirner, Kierkegaard, Richard Wagner, Bakunin, Heideg-

ger, Sartre, Camus), and the British empiricism of
Francis Bacon, Hobbes, Locke, Voltaire, Montesquieu, Hume, Bentham, John Stuart Mill, the
American pragmatists, and Bertrand Russell. It is
that evil which is unleashed by the sort of negativist arguments we have outlined above.

Man is degraded into a talking beast, a self-
evidently hermetic individuality. His individual
appetites and other hedonistic impulses are viewed
as the properties which essentially define him, and
which define, as derived constructs, the orderings
of relationships among individuals and groups of
individuals within society at large. That is the gist
of Bacon, Hobbes, Locke, Hume, and Bentham.

The doctrine of "liberty" which flows from that
immoral doctrine is the notion of the minimal
constraint by society against the uninhibited practice of individual impulses governed by the hedonistic principle of Bentham.

This is to be contrasted directly with the notion
of Freedom associated, in particular, with Apostolic Christianity.

We elaborate the point somewhat further below,
in exposing "Oxford fundamentalism" as heathen
cultism. The Christian God, like Plato's, is not a
capricious, irrational sort of anthropomorphic
Providence. The Christian God, like that of Rabbi
Philo Judaeus, Saint Peter's ally, is *a supreme
creative intelligence* which is consubstantial with a
universe undergoing continued creation in a lawful

way. That lawfulness of the process of *continuing creation* (not a *fixed* creation, in the Aristotelian sense) is represented by an ontologically real *Logos*, the Christian Holy Spirit, the Logos of the Gospel of Saint John. This Logos is the ontological reality Plato identifies with the notion of the "hypothesis of the higher hypothesis." This Logos is consubstantial with the supreme creative intelligence, and is otherwise uniquely the meaning of Reason, or the *Vernunft* which poor Immanuel Kant pronounced real, efficient, but unknowable.

Man as a mortal being is an ephemeral particularity like all discrete objects in the universe, including the beasts. However, Christianity, together with Rabbi Philo and the *Koran* as read by ibn Sina (Avicenna), distinguishes man absolutely from the beasts, by the divine quality of Reason. This is man's potential to perfect his creative intelligence to the point of discovering the lawful ordering of continuing creation, that divine quality which identifies man as in the "image of God."

On the evidence of the Apostles, Saint Paul and such leading patristics as Saint Augustine, there is no competent, honest dispute but that Christianity is *Neoplatonic*. It is essentially distinguished from Plato's dialogues only by belief in Jesus Christ's perfected divine nature. Any contrary argument is either simply misinformed or fraudulent. That point is embedded most succinctly in the Nicean Creed.

From this Apostolic Christianity flows a rigorous conception of Freedom, the notion of Freedom which informed the consciences of Benjamin Franklin and the remainder of the majority of authors of the federal Constitution of the United States.

Freedom is the action of an individual using his perfectible powers of creative intelligence to make himself an instrument of the lawful continuing creation of the universe according to Reason. Freedom is willful, joyful submission to what anarchists hate as "The Tyranny of Reason."

A more efficient approach to presenting the notion of Freedom in a systematic way is facilitated by recent progress in closer scrutiny of the work of a circle around Gaspard Monge and Lazare Carnot. This has been an ongoing, international collaboration conducted with my associates, investigations focused upon the interconnected origins of the American System of Franklin, Hamilton et al., and the progress of European continental science leading into the achievements of Riemannian physics.

Although we do not propose to burden a largely lay readership with elaborated features of modern physics, the outline of the underlying concepts of such a physics is not properly beyond the comprehension of a literate audience. Additionally, addressing an audience which emphasizes occupation with matters of military technologies, in a period when the development of "particle-beam weapons" and related apparatus is the essence of defense research-and-development concerns, that audience will not object on principle to exposure to the kinds of conceptions a citizen must master to effect competence of informed policy-judgment in such connections.

It is also important, respecting the point immediately at hand, to dispel the delusion that Apostolic Christianity is somehow in a different compartment of knowledge and belief than what is properly termed "science." As we have emphasized above, Reason is the formal quality of the Logos (Holy Spirit) of the Gospels. If the Apostles are correct on this point, as they are, the actual lawful ordering of continuing creation as a subject of scientific inquiry, is the same matter as the Logos of the Gospel. Although particular man's imperfection may leave much of this reality obscured from his comprehension, the reality persists. It persists as reality, not only in its efficiency, but in respect of its accessibility through perfection of creative intelligence. That perfection, as expressed for practice, and Freedom are one and the same matter.

Carnot on Freedom

Here we make use of added information developed by the Paris-based researches of our collaborators. The evidence obtained through primary sources enables us to prove directly what would otherwise be proven only by more elaborate forms of rigorous inference. Lazare Carnot (1753-1823) uses identical scientific methods to define the "rights of the citizen"—in contrast to the anarchist "rights of man"—and to establish the basis for the later, nineteenth-century development of the physics of functions of a multiply-connected manifold.

So, the comparison of the work of Carnot, Monge, and their immediate collaborators with the papers of Karl Weierstrass, Bernhard Riemann, and Georg Cantor leads us to a more efficient, and powerful mastery of modern, Riemannian physics than would be possible solely through the productions and unpublished papers of the German components of this development. Furthermore, just as the fallacies of Newton's physics are a direct reflection of the social notions of the empiricists Bacon, Hobbes, and Locke, so Carnot's devastating discrediting of Newton's assumptions and methods leads not only to fundamental breakthroughs in physics, but to a view of the lawful ordering of the universe which refutes the empiricist sociology of the anarchist outgrowths of empiricism.

A few highlights of Carnot's life are directly relevant to the political, as well as scientific side of the points principally under consideration in this chapter.

Carnot was a representative of a French Catholic order, the Oratorians. This order was established by Père Joseph du Tremblay and Cardinal Richelieu, as a counterforce against the powerful and dangerous Jesuit cult. Carnot's father, a close collaborator of Benjamin Franklin, as later Lazare Carnot himself, sent the youthful Lazare to study under the Oratorians, bringing the youth immediately under the continuing tutelage of Gaspard Monge.

The Oratorians were the French Catholic complement to the *politiques*, just as both were continuations of the Neoplatonic, or Augustinian current of Catholicism. This is the current which created the modern nation-state republic during the course of the fifteenth and sixteenth centuries. In addition to Tremblay and Richelieu, as well as the House of Navarre more generally, the Oratorian-*politiques* current is typified by Cardinal Mazarin and Jean-Baptiste Colbert. It was Colbert, the founder of the republican form of capitalism adopted by the creators of the United States Constitution, who coopted promising scientists, including Christian Huyghens and Leibniz, creating an opposition not only to the degenerate British Restoration Royal Society in science—and to William Petty in political economy—but also to the Jesuit-supervised René Descartes.

The master-mind for the Oratorians during the last of the seventeenth and beginning of the eighteenth centuries was Gottfried Wilhelm Leibniz.

After acknowledging his debts to his Neoplatonic predecessors, Leibniz is the nodal-point through which all subsequent genuine accomplishments in science are properly traced. This was not only a tradition of science as such, but also a political and military tradition. Not only is Leibniz almost the single-handed founder of modern science—contrary to lies taught by the British and their dupes—but the founder of the political economy adopted as the American System, and a leading spokesman for the policies of Neoplatonic natural law reflected in our Constitution and in our nation's practice of constitutional law under Chief Justice John Marshall. Leibniz not only proposed, during the seventeenth century, the breech-loading weapon and cartridge, but envisaged sweeping changes in warfare to the advantage of the republicans over the oligarchists.

Such matters are fundamentals of real history, as distinguished from the lying rubbish embedded in contemporary education and disinformed literate opinion!

It was into these circles that Carnot was placed, in opposition to the oligarchist, British-allied forces of Voltaire, Montesquieu, the Physiocrats, and the French Encyclopaedists.

In 1783, Carnot published the first edition of what became known later as his *De L'Equilibre et du Mouvement*. In 1784, he entered into direct collaboration with Benjamin Franklin. His first important military writings date from that year. This includes his "Dirigibles and Their Military Use," and his *Eloge de Vauban*. (He later developed the submarine, largely as a by-product of his military work on the dirigible, and attempted to conduit that proposal through his collaborator Fulton, to Napoleon.) That was the year he wrote for the "Reflexion sur la methaphysique du calcul infinitesimal"!

In 1788 he wrote his military-strategic work, *Memoire sur les Places Fortes*, incorporating his affirmation of the "Grand Design" policies of Henri IV and Leibniz.

In 1792, he began his rise to leadership of France, receiving his mission to reorganize the French army of the Rhine. This emerged more emphatically in 1793, with Carnot's rise to the position of what we might call today "defense minister" of the Committee of Public Safety—the vantage-point from which he overthrew the Jacobins. Carnot assembled a staff including Lindet, Prieur de la Cote d'Or, Monge, Chaptal, and Bertholet. The reorganization of the French army, begun in that year, became comprehensive with his rise to power during the Thermidorian period—beginning the summer of the following year.

The group led by Carnot developed new metallurgies, creating the light-weight, mobile artillery which played the leading role in enabling French forces to shatter every opposition, even with inferior numbers—until the events of 1812. This creation of new industries for military purposes was complemented by sweeping advances in civilian production.

Carnot also used his power to begin effecting the freedom of his ally, the Marquis de Lafayette. Lafayette was being held, on orders from William Pitt the Younger, in the Austrian dungeon at Olmütz—the affair celebrated in honor of Lafayette's wife by Beethoven's only opera, *Fidelio*. During this period, he also formed the École Polytechnique in cooperation with his former teacher and close collaborator, Gaspard Monge, while working to reestablish his alliances in the United States.

He became the contested leader of France until he was overthrown by combined British and Jesuit efforts focused through the Order of Malta agent Barras in 1797. He saved his life by fleeing to Switzerland, to join his friend and ally Lafayette. He was called back to France to head the War Ministry by Napoleon, but broke with Napoleon in 1802, opposing Napoleon's political and strategic directions.

His last public positions are notable.

In 1812, for patriotic motives, not support of Napoleon, he accepted the post as Governor of Anvers. His role there was crucial for subsequent European history. After the defeat of Napoleon, Carnot threatened to develop a defense position if

Britain moved to dismember France. The British, who rightly feared Carnot more than Napoleon in military fundamentals, relented from the proposed dismemberment of France.

Finally, in 1815, he accepted the French Interior Ministry of the "100 days," while opposing Napoleon's dedication to reopening a continental war. Chaptal was brought back by Carnot to reorganize the French economy.

He was exiled to Magdeburg in 1815, and died there in 1823.

This career in public life complements and intersects Carnot's collaboration with Monge to reinvigorate the work of Leibniz to the effect that all nineteenth-century scientific progress depends almost entirely on the accomplishments of the circles associated with the Carnots and Monge.

The coherence between Carnot's political and scientific activities is what we are emphasizing here.

Carnot centered his twofold attack on the errors of Descartes and Newton on the fallacious Newtonian assumption, Newton's borrowing from Descartes, that a body set into motion must continue with that velocity unless deterred by an intervening opposing force. Carnot's proof of the absurdity of this false assumption is the foundation of the modern theory of functions as developed by Carnot's circles, and further refined later by the influence of the overlapping work of Weierstrass,

Riemann, and Cantor in Germany. Carnot's point was directly based on Leibniz's earlier proof to the same effect.

In an actual continuum, any displacement is an alteration of the entire physical continuum; there is no empty space into which bodies can be projected as far as countervailing, intervening forces do not prevent this.

This leads to the demonstration that there is only one notion of metric associated essentially with so-called infinitesimals, *the radius of curvature of physical space* at that interval of action. Carnot extended this, as Leibniz before him, to consider the case of the indeterminacy of the infinitesimal, inclusive of the notion of immanence of a higher-order physical space at each such interval.

This investigation, furthered by Fourier, led into the notion of enumerable discontinuities of a physical function in the work of Weierstrass, Riemann, and Cantor.

This *indeterminacy* of the infinitesimal was not an *irrationalist* sort of indeterminacy. It signified that no fixed set of axiomatic assumptions concerning a specific sort of physical space could comprehend, could permit mathematical determination of the variety of existent and possible physical spaces intersecting that infinitesimal interval. Conversely, this means that a potentially enumerable number of orders of physical space, each of distinct essential characteristics, can be developed for each infinitesimal interval.

This notion corresponds to the point we made in an earlier chapter respecting the ordering of successive crucial-experimental breakthroughs in scientific knowledge.

A crucial-experimental breakthrough in scientific knowledge is distinguished from lower-order, ordinary discoveries in a fundamental way.

In the latter, there is no required alteration of existing, presumed special laws of the universe applicable to that general domain of investigative practice. The correction represented by the particular discovery is readily reconciled with the general set of axiomatic assumptions science has previously associated with its investigative practice for that special domain of inquiry.

In the former case, a crucial-experimental breakthrough, we have effects of the sort popularly associated with the introduction of the notion of general physical relativity. Our entire way of looking at entire domains of scientific inquiry is overthrown, superseded by new kinds of notions of the laws by which the universe is ordered.

Ignorant opinion, of the sort which deprecates the notion of physical relativity as a "mere theory," merely an alternative possible "explanation," ignores the most elementary facts of the matter. If we use the old assumptions, the results obtained

Karl Marx

Frederick Engels

The bearers of the Neoplatonic tradition British radicalism was created to destroy:

Gottfried Wilhelm Leibniz

Lazare Carnot

Friedrich List

Bernhard Riemann

under such information's guidances do not correspond to the consequences which must occur if the appearance of competence of the old assumptions is to be preserved. The new conceptions not only succeed in that crucial-experimental case, but prove efficiently superior as a means for investigation and experimental practice in areas in which the old assumptions were hitherto apparently unchallenged by experimental results.

Thus, we rightly insist at such points, that we must thereafter look at the world in an entirely new way, as Einstein's old teacher, Hermann Minkowski insisted back in 1907.

There are two faults with the notion of Einstein as the discoverer of physical relativity. First, the credit for what was actually accomplished is exaggerated. Einstein was among a number of preceding and contemporary thinkers who effected the breakthrough in appreciation of the experimental evidence. Second, there are gross inadequacies of assumption in the Einstein-Weyl model. Those errors centered around the attempt to analyze relativity in terms of the very incompetent sort of notion of the infinitesimal which Carnot, following Leibniz, had exposed.

Such crucial-experimental discoveries are not merely correction of previous errors. The world is not a fixed creation, of the sort which might be efficiently associated with scalar notions of elementarity. Crucial-experimental discoveries are, at least in principle, discovery of higher-order physical geometries than have been previously assumed the adequate, axiomatic notion of scientific-investigative practice. They are experimentally based insights into the existence of a higher-order domain of action within the universe as a multiply-connected manifold than has been variously either as known or as experimentally provable.

Such crucial-experimental breakthroughs express the essence of true Freedom.

Reason pertains, with respect to scientific investigation, to the fact that the universe is a multiply-connected manifold. Lawfulness in that universe is not properly associated with those axiomatic schemes which seem to adequately explain cause-and-effect in one particular domain of investigative practice. Reason—actual lawfulness—is situated with respect to the way in which the successively-ordered, interconnected domains of a manifold are ordered. Reason is transfinite with respect to anything explicable in terms of the sort of linearized "logic" associated with Newtonian physics, or with any sort of "mathematical logic."

Although few individuals in society actually make crucial-experimental breakthroughs, they employ the same qualities of creative intelligence in other ways.

First, they, in contrast to the bestial existentialists, adopt the view that the universe as a whole is coherent with a supreme creative intelligence, an intelligence which is consubstantial with that universe. Furthermore, they view the universe as a continuing process of lawful creation, not as a fixed outcome of a single past creation. They adopt the notion of Reason, as in the Christian sense of the Neoplatonic Logos. Furthermore, they seek to inform their conscience accordingly, and to make that conscience efficiently governing of their practice in all aspects of life.

This view attunes them to desiring constantly to make new discoveries, to acquire new knowledge reflecting such discoveries. They do so not only because of the benefits of such acquisitions, but because they are employing and celebrating those qualities of themselves which define them as in "the image of God."

They seek not merely the light and joy of such mental life. Knowledge is to be practiced, to prove and test itself in practice as actually knowledge of the lawful ordering of the universe. If knowledge for practice does not correspond to the Neoplatonic notion of the lawful ordering of continuing creation, then that knowledge in particular is shown to be false, a proof which demands investigation of the way the processes of judgment have been systematically spoiled to produce such mistaken prejudices.

For Carnot, in society as in the continuum, there are no self-evidently hermetic individuals. "Individual freedom" is an evil illusion. The individual is acting in the universe, through society. The individual is responsible for the consequences of both his actions and his acts of omission. There are no "individual rights"; there are only "the rights of the individual citizen."

Ethical Freedom

The individual who did not vote in the 1976 general election is as wicked, because of the inauguration of Jimmy Carter's fascist-tending regime, as the misguided dupe who actually cast a vote for Carter. The individual who did not resist the passage of PRM-32, the passage of the Reuss-sponsored act putting the nation under the sovereignty of a foreign, supranational power, is guilty of aiding to transform the United States into a fascist state.

The citizen might object to this. He or she does not concur with that characterization of Carter. He asserts that he has "a right to my own opinion" in that matter. No such "right" exists. He is as responsible for every person who dies because of his wrong opinion as if he had personally murdered each such person. There is no "right" to be wrong per se, but only the "right" of the citizen to discover truth through that democratic sort of deliberative process of interaction by which errors are corrected as a matter of knowledge, rather than by the irrationality of arbitrarily imposed correct judgments from without.

If we pursue this line of argument, then the majority of the people of the United States have been very wicked indeed—just as Christian doctrine suggests.

There is no such thing in rigorous morality as a "margin of error" between good and wickedness in judgment for practice. Either one chooses the right direction of perfecting one's judgment for practice in practice, or one is altogether wrong. There is no "right" to be wrong; there is only the wrongness of totalitarian methods of superimposing rightness. There is no proper margin of discrepancy between "ideals" and practice, but only wrong ideals and wrong practice.

Freedom is using one's creative-mental powers toward effecting innovations consistent with natural law in response to the necessary changes which natural law has made the implicit outcome of previous actions.

Freedom as the policy of a republic is the promotion of fundamental scientific and technological advances through increasing capital-intensity of productive capital in the context of compulsory public education and the nurture of the creative potentials of the individual citizen in a way consistent with that progress. This is accompanied by encouragement of the realization of the individual's creative contributions to society. These policies, as set forth in the constitutional American System of Hamilton's description, create a republican order in which those creative-mental qualities defining man as in the "image of God" order individual practice and the relationship among the citizens of that nation. It is self-development coherent with individual participation in that process which is Freedom.

Freedom is not the weakening of representative self-government, to the effect of removing the principal obstacle to a dictatorship over the nation's market and internal order by a supranational cabal of rentier finance. The notion of "free trade," of anarchist "freedom of the marketplace" is only an Orwellian fraud, slavery solicited by fools in the name of a "freedom" degraded into an empty word.

7

GNOSTICISM: 'OXFORD FUNDAMENTALISM'

Although "Oxford fundamentalism" is often shown deference even among honest, actual Christians, the fact of the matter is that it represented the insertion of a notorious sort of heathen cultism in a pseudo-Christian guise.

One should not object that the varieties of authentic Christian belief are still legitimately matters of unresolved doctrinal disputes among Christians. In respect to fundamentals—actual fundamentals—Apostolic Christianity was and remains rigorously defined historically. This distinction is most emphatically clear with respect to the adversary position of Saint Peter and other Apostles to the sort of gnostic cultism which Oxford proposed in the name of "fundamentalism."

There is a point of caution to be made. The writer was born an evangelical variety of Quaker—as distinct from the opposing, American Friends Service Committee varieties, and was raised largely in fellowship with evangelical sorts of Baptist churches. Hence, it must not be supposed that he is unfamiliar with the varieties of professed Christianity which sometimes employ the profession "fundamentalist" with rather different content. In its best usage, "fundamentalist" means one who adheres to the interpretation of the New Testament from the vantage-point of the Nicean creed—in opposition to those folk who regard various lurid, psychedelic and other heathen cults as "just another way to find God." In the evangelical churches I attended, Jimmy Carter would not be viewed as a Christian, but as merely another heathen swindler taking an obvious route in pursuit of the church-goers' vote.

How I used to shudder with revulsion—and rightly so—at each gushing pantheist who delivered a homily on the possibility of seeing God revealed through a tree or what-not. Sometimes, such romantic perversions occur in persons who are otherwise, essentially Christians, but that is no reason for calling the aberration itself "Christian."

Granted, some Sunday School-goers imagine that our access to knowledge of early, Apostolic Christianity is available only through the text of the New Testament. Nowadays, even few priests and ministers seem to have exerted themselves actually to master the wealth of historical and other material bearing on not only the events of the New Testament record, but also on the process by which the New Testament's contents were selected, and the issue of translation of each passage elaborated, with aid of various sources.

The evidence, while greatly diminished in quantity through destruction of records, is still overwhelming. Moreover, we possess not only the sort of literary evidence associated with scholarship in the narrow sense, but the most crucial points of the ordering of the Christian outlook of the Apostles and leading patristics are subject to conclusive empirical verification otherwise.

If one were to reflect on preparing a course on the essence of Christianity for otherwise well-educated persons innocent of any rigorous knowledge in the subject, my preference for a beginning would be the Gospel of Saint John. Certainly, from that starting point, everything that can be said about Christianity can be traced out in a systematic way.

"In the beginning was the Word (Logos). . ." most recall instantly. Immediately, to the scholar, that formulation, as developed through the ensuing passages, corresponds to the equivalence of Logos to Plato's notion of the "hypothesis of the higher hypothesis." In the Epistles of Saint Paul, and in the evidence of Saint John's "Revelations," the assumption is proven to be the correct one, conclusively.

This fact that Apostolic Christianity coincided in scientific method with Plato's dialogues, was a principal occupation of Apostolic and patristic

Christianity, giving rise to that qualified employment of "Neoplatonic" stipulated by Saint Augustine. Although Plotinus is not regarded strictly as a Christian authority, the gist of his commentary on Plato's *Timaeus* dialogue bears directly on the way in which the Christians defined "Neoplatonism."

Scholarship is helped on this point by the writings of the great rabbi, Philo Judaeus of Alexandria. Philo, an older contemporary of Jesus Christ and the Apostles and their ally against the paganist Sadducees and Pharisees, was also the direct ally of Saint Peter in Rome, during the fourth decade of this era, when they combined efforts against the cultist Simon ("The Magician") Magus. Moreover, on the essential methodological issues of science and theology, Philo and Apostolic Christianity concur. Both are fundamentally opposed to the method of theology and pseudoscience identifiable with the work of Aristotle.

Although, since the mid-thirteenth century, there have been stubborn efforts by some currents within the Catholic Church either to equate Aristotle's method with Christianity, or to defend Thomas Aquinas's standing by making him an "Augustinian commentator on Aristotle," there is no way in which Aristotle can be reconciled with Apostolic Christianity. The evidence is not only overwhelming, but conclusively so.

There is a slightly different problem, typified by

the common error spoiling W. Cleon Skousen's earlier *The Naked Communist* and the later *The Naked Capitalist*. In the first, he wrongly attributes communism to the hubristic "insolence" of Promethean man; in the second, he wrongly accepts the notion that John Ruskin was a Platonist, adding the popularized, but entirely wrong, British-spawned misinformation that the notion of "philosopher-king" in Plato somehow equates Plato with dictatorial proclivities.

Apostolic Christianity was and is Neoplatonic in method and essential conceptions. There is no room for contending otherwise. As we noted above, this is not merely what is proven by scholarship in the narrow sense, but also by supporting, conclusive forms of verifiable evidence apart from such literary sources.

The Christian God, like the God of the Judaism of Philo, is not an anthropomorphic God, but a supreme creative intelligence, consubstantial with the universe so ordered. This supreme being is accessible to human empirical knowledge through the Logos (Holy Spirit). The Logos is an ontological reality, which is defined in form by Plato's notion of the "hypothesis of the higher hypothesis." Among the ephemeral, particular actualities of the universe, man is distinguished as in the "image of God" by his potential powers of creative intelligence, the power to discover the higher lawful ordering of a continuing process of creation through ordering his own labor according to discoveries effected by man's potential creative intelligence.

That power of mankind, which sets him above the beasts, is therefore divine, as it partakes of the universal, and is thus distinct from the ephemeral, beastlike mortality of the human biology otherwise. In the perfection of that divine quality of potential for creative intelligence, man comes into agreement with the real ordering of the universe, the Logos, and thus achieves atonement with the Logos and the supreme being which is consubstantial with the Logos.

What distinguishes Christianity from the Judaism of Rabbi Philo Judeaus is none of the foregoing considerations. The distinction, as set forth by the Gospel of Saint John and other parts of the Gospels, is the uniqueness of Jesus Christ as perfected in his divine nature.

The doctrine of Christianity is the "imitation of Christ" through perfecting one's conscience, through the development of creative intelligence, to so govern one's practice. The duty of man is to be the instrument of God through practice determined by the process of perfection of his powers of creative intelligence.

The mortality of individual man locates the realization of this process of perfection not in the individual as such, but through the body of mankind generally, the Church in the broadest sense of such a community. So, the act of creative intelligence is to perfect the knowledge of others for practice, and to receive the same quality of gifts that others contribute in a like manner. So, creative discovery, sometimes likened in quality to a "light turning on inside the head," is associated with the lovingness of such relations of sharing knowledge for practice.

This general arrangement intersects the process defined by the three qualities of existence possible for the individual. Those three qualities are examined in depth by Dante Alighieri in his *Commedia*.

They are, summarily, as follows.

On the lowest level, man is like an egoistical, irrational infant. He is all sensual appetites, his morality at best one of propitiating his mother, with emphasis always on the possessive pronoun "mine." He is, in summary, an anarchist, an existentialist—he is evil.

On the next, higher level, man seeks rationality of cause-and-effect in the world. He asks "How?" and "Why?" He considers the ultimate consequences for himself and for others generally in respect to his acts of omission, as well as his explicit actions. He struggles to inform his conscience morally, and shapes his conscience by meditating on the whole of his life, between birth and death, seeking to make that whole worthy of having existed. Yet, he is imperfect in conscience. He is preoccupied with goals of "earthly paradise," with rewards to be enjoyed within his moral life-time. He is a creature from the "Purgatory" of Dante's *Commedia.* Although he wishes to do nothing which violates the worthiness of his life as a whole, his conscience must constantly wrestle, often defeated, with contrary, short-term impulses of appetite and prejudice, suffering a constant torment in the conflict between the purpose of his entire life and the impulse to acquire "earthly paradise."

On the third, highest, level, he is transformed. Instead of his conscience serving as a constraint over his search for "earthly paradise," his mortal being becomes an instrument for that which is divine, the development of his potential creative intelligence for a universal purpose.

It is so in the Judaism of Rabbi Philo Judaeus. It is so in the *Koran* of the Prophet Mohammed, as that was correctly comprehended on this point by ibn Sina (Avicenna). Hence, having in common a rejection of a heathen, anthropomorphic notion of God, in favor of a supreme creative intelligence, and ordering the matter otherwise in agreement, actual Apostolic Christianity, the Judaism of Philo, and the *Koran* as read by ibn Sina represent a form of fellowship known as ecumenicism.

Except for the indicated concurrences and differences among Christianity, Philo's Judaism, and ibn Sina's Islam, the remaining difference within and among them is properly a matter of ministries,

the adopted disciplines, including matters of fast-
ing periods, and so forth, which are adopted to
aid the individual in overcoming the kinds of problems associated, especially, with the outline given
in the first two canticles of Dante's *Commedia*.

All pseudo-Christianity either adopts or implicitly adopts an anthropomorphic God in place of
the Christian supreme creative intelligence, and
either rejects the notion of the Logos (Holy Spirit)
entirely or supplants it with the psychopathologi-
cal symptoms of a *Schwärmerei*. Such supplanta-
tions define the forms of pseudo-Christianity
which are termed "charismatic."

Such deformations have not erupted sponta-
neously. Like gnosticism, Arianism, Manicheanism, and Donatism, the perversions associated with
Oxford's religious undertakings have all been wittingly introduced for a malignant purpose by
agents of an overall grouping of cults identified
principally by the Mesopotamian "magicians," the
cult of Apollo, and the Ptolemaic form of the cult
of Isis-Osiris-Horus. It is not coincidental that the
branch of the river Thames proximate to Oxford
is named the Isis.

The principal mediator of such cultist practices
into Western European culture has been a group
of ancient Rome's senatorial families, which has
maintained over approximately 2000 years their
forebears' dedication to the two official cults of

pagan Rome, the Cult of Apollo, which ruled Rome during the historical republican period, and the "mystery" cult of Isis, established under the Caesars. Since the sixteenth century, the principal mediator of those cultist practices has been the agents of the black nobility deployed under the cover of the Jesuits.

Oxford and Cambridge universities since the middle-to-latter part of the sixteenth century have been adjuncts of the Jesuit order, and the inner circle of the Church of England hierarchy, including the hierarchy of the Anglican Cathedral of St. John the Divine in New York City, has been engaged, in collaboration with evil circles of the Jesuits, in spawning pseudo-Christian and even more lurid cults in service of the cults of Apollo and Isis.

Oxford fundamentalism was just such a Jesuitical project.

The Method of the Pseudo-Christian Fundamentalism

The Jesuit method is Aristotelian in the sense that Aristotle himself was an agent of the cult of Apollo at Delphi, deployed as a Persian spy into Athens through the Apollo cult's chief conduit there, the school of rhetoric of Isocrates. Hence, the adopted name for the modern Jesuit method is the "delphic method."

The alternate name for the "delphic method" is *nominalism,* which is otherwise the method of British empiricism—quite consistent with the Jesuit affiliations of the founder of the British empiricist school, the pederast Francis Bacon.

The structural features of Aristotelian logic betray the characteristics of the nominalist method. In that deductive procedure, the position of "cause" in reality is replaced by the mere copula connecting the middle terms of the syllogism. The mere names of things are substituted for the reality of things named, and the link through middle terms of syllogistic forms of mere rhetoric is substituted, in the name of rigorously logical argument, for reason.

The principle of rhetoric is this. By stripping the reality of process away from the names and formulations used to label such processes, new meanings can be attached to those names and formulations by charismatic methods—the aspect of the term "rhetoric" that predominates in current usage today.

The classic illustration of the application of this method of fraud is Aristotle's perverted commentary on Plato's *Timaeus* dialogue.

The Jesuit trick is to either repeat the words used by an intended victim of such frauds, or to slightly paraphrase such terminology. The Jesuit then reduces the terms to his paranoid sort of deductive analysis, and reaches for charismatic sophistries to attach to that analysis entirely different meanings.

That is the Jesuit trick with the Bible used to develop "delphic" pseudo-Christianities in the name of "fundamentalism."

Start with the assertion: The Bible is the Word of God. This is a fraud, since "Word" means Logos or Holy Spirit, which the words in the Gospels are supposed to reflect, not embody.

Now, having freed the words in the Bible from their substance, the Jesuit has degraded those words into mere words.

This involves a problem for the Jesuit, since it is documented beyond contrary argument that not only were the contents of the Bible carefully selected over centuries of disputed labor, but that the question of authentic source-documents and translations has never been resolved. The Bible, especially the New Testament, was compiled on the basis of evidence that the selected texts were consistent with the body of Apostolic Christianity as a whole.

The Jesuit works his way around this considerable difficulty by a rhetorician's trick, asserting it actually or proximately to blasphemy to presume that God would permit anything to be included in the particular version of the Bible in view which was not His literal intent.

Having affected the separation of the Bible text from the substance of Christianity, the Jesuit or like corrupter proceeds to attach his own meanings, with aid of homilies, to each passage. The result defies reason when taken as a self-contradictory whole. No matter: "It is a mystery"!

For an extreme case of such cultism, compare the most extreme sort of pseudo-Islamic doctrine, that of the Oxford-created Muslim Brotherhood. The consistent adherent of the Brotherhood would argue as follows:

He is encountered holding a loaded gun to the head of his wife. The onlooker warns, "Be careful; if you pull that trigger, you will kill your wife!"

The Brother solemnly rebukes that infidel of an onlooker: "The bullet can not kill unless Allah has willed it to be so."

The essential common feature of Oxford fundamentalists, Muslim Brotherhood or otherwise, is that God is an anthropomorphic, irrational being, like one of the gods of Olympus. This pagan's god rules the universe by caprice. The individual, therefore, is not responsible for the efficient consequences of his acts or acts of omission in the world.

This is related to the superstition known as gambling: worship of the pagan Goddess Fortuna. It is related to the evil cult known as astrology, or the related practices of the cult of Delphi, or of the Isis cult.

In fact, it degrades the believer to the lowest of the canticles in Dante's *Commedia*.

"Logic" Versus "Reason"

One of the essential concomitants of such productions of pseudo-Christian cults is the stated or essentially implied equation of "reason" with mere "logic." By demonstrating the inadequacies of mere logic, the sophist Jesuit denies the universality of Reason.

Since the physics of Newton et al. is a neo-Aristotelian fraud, "force" in Newtonian physics has the significance only of the copula in Aristotelian logic. Hence, the fact that Newtonian and similar forms of inorganic physics are demonstrably inadequate can be used either to show that Newton's method is wrong, or, if one asserts Newton's authority for science, then one has argued that reality lies outside science. By equating "reason" to mere "logic," the manufacturers of sophistical homilies assert the higher authority of the irrational, or of the charismatic.

The fraud involved is essentially as follows.

Earlier, in reviewing the case of successive crucial-experimental breakthroughs in scientific knowledge, we emphasized the importance of adopting the relationship among such crucial-experimental revolutions in scientific knowledge as true and fundamental with respect to the inferior sort of ordinary scientific knowledge located in the intervals between such points.

The characteristic subsuming such an ordering of crucial-experimental breakthroughs has the physical-mathematical significance of "transfinite" in the sense associated with the discoveries of Georg Cantor as applied to Riemannian physics.

There are, in reality, hierarchies of such transfinites in the actual organization of the universe, a fact which gives empirical basis for the notion of the universe as a self-elaborating complex of multiply-connected manifoldness. Each domain of such a manifold is associated with a *characteristic principle of action.* This, if empirically adduced correctly, permits us to achieve deterministic knowledge of most of the outcomes of cause-effect relationship within that domain. These characteristics, each transfinite with respect to the ordering it subsumes, belong to an ordering of such characteristics. That ordering of characteristics (hypothesis), in turn reflects a higher-order transfinite (higher hypothesis). The notion of the "hypothesis of the higher hypothesis," so defined by Plato, is equivalent to the notion of hypothesis in Riemann's physics of a multiply-connected manifold.

It is the notion of the "hypothesis of the higher hypothesis" which is equivalent to the notion of reason in the Platonic/Neoplatonic sense, to the form, as distinct from the ontological reality, of the Logos. In Plato, as in his *Timaeus* dialogue, the ontological reality of the "hypothesis of the higher hypothesis" is situated in its consubstantiality with the supreme creative intelligence consubstantial with the universe as a whole.

Logic, by comparison, is mere description of the phenomena which lie below the level of the lowest strata of hypothesis. Logic is man's imitation of the soulless empirical knowledge of the beasts.

In Christianity, there are no absolute mysteries, but only ignorance, lack of perfection of the powers of efficient creative reason. This deficiency is more emphatic with respect to the infantile mind. The anarchist, the existentialist, cannot comprehend because his mind is too degraded morally to conceive of reason. Since the existentialist can neither smell, nor eat, nor fornicate with reason, it does not exist for him.

The person on the level of "Purgatory," is so attached to sensuous objects as objects of possession that their ephemeral nature he must deny. Reason affects his conscience, but he can not accept the ontological reality of reason without first surrendering his last infantilist fascination with the object of possession as fundamental. In terms of physics, phase-space notions are extraordinarily difficult for him.

This problem is better analyzed by examining the problem Kant sets for himself in his *Critique of Pure Reason*. He finds reason to exist, and efficiently, but defines it as unknowable. His difficulty, as we find most efficiently by studying his shorter *Critique of Practical Reason*, is that Kant lived out his life in a state of Purgatory. The proof of this point is a short book in itself, a proof I have summarized in other published locations. It is, however, sufficient to the point at hand to report it here as I have done.

The direct perception of reason, in Kant's sense of pure reason, is possible only for persons developing to the third level, the "Paradise" of Dante's *Commedia*.

The reader should refer his attention, once again, to the earlier discussion of the points of crucial-experimental breakthroughs. Once one comprehends a succession of breakthroughs as an ordered set of actualities, and grasps the notion of the relative transfinite, the characteristics of such an ordering, the notion of transfiniteness has been comprehended. This permits the extension of the application of such a notion to empirically demonstrable, efficient higher transfinite orderings.

This conception requires shifting the geometry of one's thinking-processes, away from the false preoccupation with the assumed self-evidence of the existent particular object. A case in point was Erwin Schroedinger's use of Riemannian physics, the physics of the multiply-connected manifold, to define the electron as a "wavicle," as a particular existence whose existence is not self-evident, but determined.

That shift in thinking occurs among scientists in the way suggested by the cited illustration. Once the scientist grasps the fact that it is the successive revolutions in scientific knowledge which are the only fundamental reality of scientific activity as a whole, the scientist is impelled toward the correlated discovery that the creative aspect of his own mental powers is correlated with the self-elaboration of the sort of transfinite, efficient principle which orders such successive, crucial-experimental breakthroughs. Rather than being preoccupied, in the egotistical sense of discovery, with particular discoveries, the scientist now comes to view particular discoveries as the mere predicates of a process of conscious mastery of the relative transfinite which orders successive breakthroughs of a crucial-experimental significance. He shifts his focus of scientific work, to seek out and willfully direct his efforts toward a next order of such crucial-experimental hypothesis. Therewith, he abandons the notions of science he learned as a schoolboy, and orders his thinking about science according to this newly acquired outlook.

So, the person who has made the potential powers of creative intelligence the object of perfection subordinates the particular in his or her individual life to the task of effecting the power to make new crucial-experimental-like breakthroughs. These hypotheses become for him or her the increased power of perfection mediated to mankind generally, and his or her existence has so been comprehended more or less efficiently as an ephemeral instrument of reason.

This defines, of course, the circumstances under

which reason, the lawful ordering of the universe, remains inaccessible to persons on the first and second of the levels outlined. Hence, for them *the very idea of reason remains a mystery.*

It is not intrinsically a mystery. It is their clinging, so to speak, to their existentialist or ambivalent preoccupation with a narrow view of their sensuous mortality which blinds them to an otherwise intrinsically, accessible actuality.

The work of Christianity is to order society according to that knowledge. The persons on the two lower levels are sheep, who lack the developed mental powers to lead themselves to safety. They must be led. Their consciences must be informed of the truth, or at least the shadow of the truth, so that they are saved despite their imperfect condition. This is accomplished by the shepherds, those who have entered into the condition Dante locates in the "Paradise" canticle of his *Commedia.* The apostolic conception, the notion of the body of the Christian church, constantly developing qualified shepherds in each generation, is integral to this.

To the Apostolic Christian, Jesus Christ saved the world from the doom intrinsic to the Isis cult-ruled order of the Roman empire, through his martyrdom to the end of creating the Christian church as a continuing body. The instrument for that work was prescribed to be the Logos (Holy Spirit), the instrument of reason—in the true sense of reason—which was inaccessible to mankind in its general extant condition in any other way. So, although the truth was conveyed, in Saint Paul's Platonic usage, "as through a glass darkly," it might be efficiently conveyed.

As much as need be said to the point at hand is now said.

The evil we combat is otherwise to be seen as organized irrationalism, like that of the literally satanic Muslim Brotherhood of Ayatollah Khomeini's followers and co-thinkers. Just as the source of ancient Asharism, like the British-created neo-Asharite varieties converging into the Muslim Brotherhood, was created by the Egypt-based cult of Isis, so the irrationalistic cults of pseudo-Christian Oxford fundamentalism are similarly productions of the same authorship. Ayatollah Khomeini and the Reverend Jim Jones are siblings of the same mother, Isis. These are modern Donatist-like spawn of gnostic Manicheanism, the evil adversaries Saint Peter and Rabbi Philo joined forces to combat at Rome.

8

WHO IS ISIS?

To Apostolic Christianity, Isis is the Egyptian name for the Whore of Babylon, just as Satan is the semitic name for Dionysus.

For what are these evil creatures, Apollo, Isis, and the deities of the Mesopotamian magicians, the representatives, apart from Nero, Caligula, and their descendants among the black nobility of Europe today?

British-Jesuit "communism" and British-Jesuit cultist concoctions of anthrosophy and Oxford fundamentalism are created to the purpose of forming social battering rams against republican order. They are formed from the superstitious poor, which have been left as strata in a condition of existentialist infantilism. They are recruited from among adolescents, through procedures as ancient as the cult of Dionysus. What is the policy of that adversary who spawns such monstrous concoctions?

The issue is most efficiently defined by turning our attention to the eastern Mediterranean of the fourth century B.C.

The world of that period was divided between a faction of allied forces of the Babylonians, the Isis cult, and the cult of Apollo, on the one side, and the forces led by Plato's Academy at Athens, on the other.

The adversaries of Plato, marshalled in the rulership of the Persian Empire, were determined to destroy the republican faction forever. This was to be accomplished by means of a project for splitting the Persian Empire into two parts. One part would persist to the east of the Euphrates. The second part, "the Western Division," was to be based in the area to the west of the Euphrates, and to engulf all of the Mediterranean.

The instrument chosen for this project was Philip of Macedon. Philip was first to absorb all of Greece, which represented the only efficient military technology of the period. Philip was to carve out the Western Division with his enlarged forces, and proceed from there.

The form of society to be constructed was known in the literature of that period as either the "Persian model" or the "oligarchical model."

The essence of the model was this. The principle of the urban-centered republican order was to be extirpated from society once and for all. Society was to be essentially ruralized, except for cities as administrative entities. It was to be an order of rural-oriented, labor-intensive "zero technological growth," with the masses of people kept in moral subjugation through fragmentation, cultivated backwardness, and cults. It was to be a "one world of regions," ruled by a feudal-like oligarchy, something like Huxley's "Brave New World."

Acting through Alexander the Great, the forces of Plato's Academy almost defeated the oligarchists. However, Alexander's death by poisoning enabled the oligarchists around the key figure of Ptolemy and Aristotle's Peripatetics to prevail. So, the world declined into obscenity prior to the appearance of Christ and Christianity.

The oligarchists were never fully defeated. Radiating from the Isis-cultists who often controlled the papacy from their vantage-point as the hereditary senatorial families of Rome, they today represent an axis of power centered around the organizations of the European black nobility and the rentier-financier axis running from Genoa through Geneva, Amsterdam, and London, into Manhattan, and strongly supplemented by the financial power of the drug-traffic centers of Hong Kong, Bangkok, Singapore, and the British West Indies.

That is the secret of the "One World" ferment, including the Aspen Institute, the New York Council on Foreign Relations, the Bilderbergs, and the Heritage Foundation subsidiary of the Mont Pelerin Society, plus Georgetown University.

These forces, united generally around the Club of Rome's proposals for a "new dark age," and genocide to reduce the world's population levels by billions over the coming two decades, are determined to wipe out capitalist republicanism for once and for all during the closing decades of this century.

Why Are They Plotting War Against Russia?

Since pot-puffing fops of the likes of William F. Buckley are kook-cultists up to their eyeballs in this "libertarian" one-world venture, why are they plotting war against the Soviet Union once again?

On this point, the beliefs of most conservatives break down into absurdity.

They certainly have no objection to communism. It is the Jesuits who run the Communist Party of Mexico topdown, as well as continuing to exert potent influence over Fidel Castro. It is the British crowd which controls the Communist Party, U.S.A. topdown, as well as the entire assortment of "environmentalists" and other "leftists" of the United States today, all the way through to the terrorists.

They do not object to "communism" as most conservatives associate communism with the CPUSA or Communist Party of Mexico. After all, they created and control such entitites. They object to *industrialized Russia*, not to Communist Russia, just as they did at the beginning of this century.

The *1980s Project* papers of the New York

Council on Foreign Relations are clear on this point. Those papers, authored under the supervision of Cyrus Vance, W. Michael Blumenthal, Brzezinski and others, are published by McGraw-Hill, with aid of a grant from the Lilly Endowment. No conservative has any excuse disputing my report on this account.

The argument of the Council is that the main enemy of the United States is a threatened revival of the "mercantilist" form of nationalist economic policy associated with Alexander Hamilton and Friedrich List. Does that not pique your sense of irony? The American System, for whose establishment our forefathers fought the American Revolution, is in some magical way to be deemed the principal enemy of the United States?

Whence comes this danger? According to the CFR, echoing forces in Britain, the danger flows from the alliance of Gaullist France with West Germany, to the effect of creating a new, gold-based monetary system fulfilling the economic policies of Hamilton and List. In other words, the danger seen by the CFR is that France, West Germany, and other nations will successfully impose the system establishing by the Founding Fathers of the United States upon most of the world.

How do they propose to fight this alleged danger to the United States, the danger posed by the founding fathers of the United States? By destroying Soviet Russia!

How does this connect, even in so twisted a mind as that of Brzezinski? The danger is that economic cooperation between France and Germany, on the one side, and Moscow on the other, would make France and Germany so strong that the effort to put the world under an American System might succeed. Therefore, by destroying Russia, France, Germany, and Japan could be easily crushed.

That is precisely the CFR's argument.

That is the policy of that grinning, mentally-unbalanced rhesus monkeylike figure, Jimmy Carter; that is the policy of Ronald Reagan's Georgetown Jesuit advisers. Do you propose that your choice is between a lunatic Carter, controlled by a probably more lunatic Kissinger and Brzezinski or a good-hearted but dumb Reagan, controlled by that gaggle of lunatic Jesuits?

What Would Be the Outcome?

Momentarily, the next move for the Soviets is to proceed with military occupation of the Western desert portion of Communist China, Sinkiang, thus effectively reducing China's strategic military capabilities to below zero. Whether or when that might occur is not be to predicted. That is the next crucial strategic move for which Moscow is presently deployed.

Give Peking modern booster and targeting capability? Brezhnev reviewed that prospect with a high-level emissary recently. "We shall destroy

China's nuclear capability with bombardment,"
Brezhnev said, "and the United States will have
thirty minutes to decide on fighting World War
III or not!" That is no bluff; that is Moscow's
present mood, and is the clearly indicated unique
response to such a situation.

Similarly, the placement of Pershing II missiles
in Western Europe now means instant World War
III.

Contrary to the wishful nonsense about Soviet
technological inferiority, Soviet military capabilities are effectively in excess of NATO's, and this
margin will grow rapidly during the coming twelve
months, becoming a qualitative margin with the
deployment of particle-beam weapons. New Soviet
laser weaponry has made the Cruise missile obso-
lete before it is yet deployed.

The point, generally, is that CFR policy has put
the United States and the Western Alliance overall
into a downward spiral, from which there is no
escape except by U.S. cooperation with France
and Germany to put the new, gold-based world
monetary system into immediate operation.

In short, the position of the United States will
become increasingly indefensible as long as the
present Anglo-American geopolitical policy persists in any form, including that of the most arms-
prone elements of the Committee on the Present
Danger.

The solution is to rally the crisis-wracked majority of the American electorate in an upsurge of American nationalism, around the central policy-theme of joining with the European Monetary System to establish immediately the new, gold-based monetary system which I first proposed in April 1975 as the International Development Bank. That proposal has been made an imminent reality by the European Monetary System, and would be an assured reality with cooperation of a new President dedicated to such a result.

Having ordered the affairs of most of the world by adoption of such a policy, we shall deal with Moscow by treating it as the representative of industrialized Russia, not as Communist Russia. To make short of a point, Moscow will accept that, and we shall have thereby secured our nation for our posterity.

The question is, do we have the intelligence and courage to bring this about quickly, at whatever cost? Or, by failing to do just that, have we demonstrated that 2,000 years of Christendom shall go down the drain because we lack the moral qualities of intelligence and courage which constitute our nation's moral fitness to survive?